The Retirement Diaries®

Gwynneth Mary Lovas

Copyright © 2016 Gwynneth Mary Lovas

NOTICE AND DISCLAIMER: All rights reserved. No part of this publication may be reproduced, stored in a retrieval system, or transmitted, in any form or by any means, electronic, mechanical, photocopying, recording or otherwise, without the prior written consent of Gwynneth Mary Lovas.

This book is a work of fiction. Names, characters, places and incidents either are products of the author's imagination or are used fictitiously. Any resemblance to actual events or locales or persons, living or dead, is entirely coincidental.

No one involved in this publication is attempting herein to render legal, accounting or other professional advice. If legal, accounting or other professional or expert assistance is required, the services of a competent professional should be sought.

ISBN: 978-0-9958170-0-5

The Retirement Diaries® and The Retirement Fairy® are registered trademarks of Gwynneth Mary Lovas.

theretirementdiaries.com
theretirementfairy.com

For Steven

CONTENTS

Acknowledgments ... viii
Introduction ... ix

1. Debacle Avoidance ... 1
2. Timing Is Everything ... 7
3. Deutschland, Deutschland, Uber Alles ... 8
4. Decisions, Decisions ... 10
5. Malignant Glaucoma ... 13
6. Respect ... 15
7. Netflix: The Opiate of the Masses ... 17
8. Practically Romantic ... 19
9. Beyond The Pale ... 20
10. Dirty Jobs ... 22
11. Blue In Hawaii ... 23
12. Twink ... 27
13. Are They Kidding? ... 28
14. The Sound of Silence ... 29
15. *Tempus Fugit* ... 32
16. Orbit City ... 35
17. Hippity-Hoppity ... 37
18. Cash For Trash ... 40
19. The Lyrics Paradigm ... 43
20. The "Returns" Counter ... 44
21. *Siddhartha* Revisited ... 48
22. Extra! Extra! ... 50
23. To Dream Or Not To Dream ... 51
24. What Did You Say? ... 52
25. There Is A God ... 55
26. Joey, Joey, Bo Boey ... 58
27. And Now The Shipping News ... 60
28. Sudden-Onset Ass Expansion ... 61
29. Fill 'Er Up ... 63
30. Bzzzz ... 64
31. Valhallaland ... 66
32. The Sword Of Damocles ... 71
33. Guerrilla Gardening ... 73
34. Hold The Onions ... 75

35. Mirror, Mirror ... 77
36. Life Without Parole ... 79
37. The Oracle ... 80
38. Do You See What I See? ... 83
39. Suzy Homemaker ... 85
40. Fine Young Cannibals ... 87
41. TMI ... 89
42. Pick A Spot; Any Spot ... 91
43. Velcro Sandals ... 93
44. Independence Day ... 95
45. Farting Barbie ... 99
46. Goldfish ... 100
47. Let There Be Light ... 101
48. 98.9° ... 102
49. Mao Revisited ... 104
50. Take Two Aspirin ... 106
51. Ninja Granny ... 108
52. Come Fly With Me ... 112
53. Please Fasten Your Seatbelts ... 114
54. Akimbo ... 116
55. Surprise! ... 119
56. Twilight Zone ... 121
57. Old Dog. New Tricks. ... 122
58. So It's Come To This... ... 125
59. Pillemma ... 126
60. Mastermind ... 128
61. Dream Maker ... 130
62. Spot Cleaning ... 133
63. Older vs. Old ... 135
64. Ooh...Sparkles! ... 139
65. Just When You Thought You Were Out ... 142
66. Napping Injuries ... 144
67. Metamorphosis ... 146
68. Be Kind. Rewind. ... 148
69. "The Eagle Has Landed" ... 151
70. One Ringy-Dingy ... 155
71. Jedi Mind Trickery ... 157
72. Seventy-Two Hours ... 161
73. More Schmancy Than Fancy ... 163

74. Hocus Bogus ... 166
75. Would You Like Fries With That? ... 167
76. Tricky Treat ... 168
77. Things That Make You Go "Aah" ... 170
78. Desert Island Game ... 172
79. Sure, But Can You Dance? ... 174
80. Home, Home Without A Range ... 175
81. Aaargh! *&%$# ... 177
82. Bad Juju ... 178
83. Nomenclature ... 179
84. Cheers! ... 181
85. How Many Is That? ... 184
86. Will That Be In A Cup Or A Bowl? ... 186
87. How Sweet It Is ... 188
88. Pass The Pretzels ... 190
89. O Holy Night ... 193
90. Bienvenue ... 196
91. Down To Two ... 197
92. Are You The Beef Or The Rack Of Lamb? ... 198
93. Have You Got Me On Speaker? ... 201
94. The Aging Aquarius ... 203
95. Time To Say Goodbye ... 205
96. Ouch! ... 207
97. Man vs. Fridge ... 209
98. Trouble In River City ... 212
99. How To Recognize That You Are Retired ... 214
100. *Annus Horribilis?* ... 216

About the Author ... 220

Gwynneth Mary Lovas

ACKNOWLEDGMENTS

I would like to acknowledge the many people who have supported my efforts in writing this book through their encouragement and advice, and whose humor has inspired me. In particular, I want to thank my husband, Steven Lovas, Peter Turner, Katherine Blake, Corinne Sceviour, Alan and Tamara Lovas, Gary Seymour, Steven Turner and Matthew Turner. Special thanks to my mother, Elizabeth Turner, who listened tirelessly to countless hours of re-reads over the telephone…and still laughed.

INTRODUCTION

SO YOU ARE PLANNING ON RETIRING, and you're pretty sure that retirement will be like a never-ending summer holiday; that every night will feel like Saturday night.

Or, perhaps you imagine enjoying long hours pondering such mysteries of the universe as dark energy and string theory, with that same smile etched on your face that comes every fall when you get to set the clocks back an hour.

Well, in a perfect world, all of the above would be true. But for most of us, retirement probably falls somewhere between our daydreams and trying not to think too much about everything that can go wrong during cataract surgery.

Somewhat akin to a vacation with the kids that goes on just a little too long, a happy retirement doesn't come quite as naturally as you might think. Ironically, retirement requires work. That's right, if you want to succeed at being retired, you are going to have to work at it.

I'm not saying you should give up on your retirement dreams, I'm simply saying that retirement plans should come with a warning label: "Some Assembly Required". And, while each of us will have different experiences, we probably share more than you might think.

With that in mind, I invite you to take a peek into the personal diaries of a new retiree, to give you a little taste of just how strangely different from your expectations your first year of retirement can be…

1. DEBACLE AVOIDANCE

Saturday, February 6

Dear Diary:

Well, today was it, day one of my retirement. So how do I feel? On the whole, today has been pretty much anticlimactic. I'm wondering if maybe the dream of retirement was a lot better than retirement itself; very *Ode on a Grecian Urn*.

But maybe achieving any goal in life is never quite as great as the pursuit:

"Yeah, graduating from college was a pretty proud moment ... would you like fries with that?"

"Of course we wanted everything to be super special. We spent four years planning and fifty thousand dollars on our wedding... What honey? Just use toilet paper. I told you we ran out of Kleenex!"

"Naturally, I was really excited about having my first baby...Will you stop crying already? I just fed you!"

The truth is that yesterday, my last day of work, was actually much more special. Aside from the fact that it was my birthday, it felt pretty awesome to know that I would never have to fill out another staff survey, attend another annual conference, sit through one more employee evaluation or fill out another leave request. Moreover, my retirement lunch was at a great restaurant and there were lots of nice things said. The only awkward part for me was receiving gifts in front of everybody. Some people always manage to be gracious about receiving gifts. I am not one of those people. I do not like surprises. People who know me always check with me in advance about birthday and Christmas gifts. If I open up a gift and find a sparkly burgundy sweater inside, I'm just as likely to say, "I don't like this," as "Thank you so much."

Fortunately, most of the gifts I received were more or less what you would expect for a retirement and I was able to pull off "gracious acceptance". But for one or two of them, there was an awkward pause before I managed to formulate the words, "Thank you." It's not like it ruined the party or anything, there was just a temporary uncomfortable shuffling of feet and low murmuring.

Which brings me to my point. I think somebody should create a "Dos and Don'ts" list for retirement gift giving. Nobody, neither the giver nor the receiver, wants to be responsible for actually killing an otherwise perfectly enjoyable event. A retirement party shouldn't end with the music and laughter stopping, a pall of silence falling over the room and people wandering back to the office because the thought of work is suddenly more appealing than the debacle that your party has become. So I have taken it upon myself to put together this bit of honest advice for people who are wondering what to get for someone as a retirement gift:

What Not To Give:
    1. Flowers - Unless you are in a romantic relationship with the retiree, think long and hard before you decide to give flowers. Flowers can suggest that you are thinking "We decided to give you some flowers now ... you know ... while you are still alive." A retirement party should never feel like a funeral.
    2. Plants - Giving a plant virtually screams, "Oh, I thought this was for a house warming." And a plant is not a gift. A plant is a responsibility. They are immortal. If you don't kill them, they will last forever. There are trees that are thousands of years old. So if you are still considering giving a plant, you might as well just go all out and give the retiree a puppy.
    3. Plaques - In short, a plaque pretty much says, "We want you to remember us long after we have forgotten you." Here is the unexpurgated truth. Nobody wants a plaque. Nobody ever hangs a plaque up on a wall at home. A plaque can't be sold in a garage sale. You can't even give a plaque away. Hint - if something has no value to anyone else on the planet, then it has no value to the person who is retiring. And if Edna in Human Resources is hurt because it was her idea, you know what to get her when she retires.
    4. Coffee-Table Books - Most of us download the books we want onto our Kindles and Kobos and iPads. We use our coffee tables for putting our feet up or eating our dinner while we watch CNN or Netflix. We have no use for coffee table books. We have no interest in Beautiful Banff, Coco Chanel or the History of Iceland. We will put that book in the trunk of our car. It will stay there. We will never think about it again. At best, it will provide convenient traction for a tire that's stuck in the mud.

5. Money - As practical a gift as money may at first blush appear to be, bear in mind that the retiree is not "graduating" from their job. While a crisp bill in a card may say "Congratulations on your wonderful achievement" to an eighteen-year-old, to a retiree it ends up saying something more along the lines of "I hear you don't have a job anymore. Hope this helps." There is no way around it. Cash is weird.

6. Watches - The right watch presented by a corporation to a retiring employee says, "We value the time you spent here." Think Piaget, Franck Muller, Patek Philippe, Chopard, Rolex or Omega. Anything less says, "Oh, you're retiring. We found this in the storage closet. You can have it." From the staff or an individual, a watch is never a great idea unless you can afford one of the "good" ones or the retiree has specifically asked for a cheap watch, which almost never occurs.

7. Anything from a Craft Fair - Anything from a craft fair is not an acceptable retirement gift. It is the equivalent of giving your Mom a birdhouse made of Popsicle sticks when you are thirty-seven years old. In fact, since we are on the subject, anything from a craft fair is not an acceptable gift for anybody on any occasion. There. I said it. We all know it's true.

8. DVDs and CDs - Much like books, people tend to download what they really want for themselves. There is only one possible exception to this advice, a Complete Series Box Set of *The Sopranos*, *Breaking Bad* or *The Wire*. Do not deviate from this list under any circumstances, even if your sister saw something else that she said was "really good". Nothing else is that good. Word. A note of caution – if the person retiring has ever talked about Jesus at work, the exception does not apply.

What To Give:

1. Chocolates - If you want to say a personal "best wishes" to a friend or colleague, a box of chocolates is a good choice. Everybody loves chocolates. Nobody ever buys themselves a box of chocolates. Best of all, people have been known to dig as greedily into a box of Russell Stover's or Black Magic as a box of Godiva or Debauve & Gallais. However, if you are in charge of selecting the gift from the entire staff, chocolates may only be given in combination with another gift.

2. Alcohol - You simply can't go wrong with alcohol. Ever. Booze is the universally appreciated gift. Even teetotalers can re-gift a bottle of booze. Neither does the retiree have to be a wine aficionado or into drinking rare scotch – everybody likes to party. Giving a bottle of booze doesn't say, "We all think you're an alcoholic," it says, "We want you to enjoy your retirement." Give a vintage wine or a bottle of Champagne and you will always be remembered fondly. Cheers.

3. Pens - Subject to limited qualifications, a pen can be a superb retirement gift. The pen cannot be plastic. The pen cannot have your company logo on it. The pen cannot come in a box with eleven other pens exactly like it. The pen should not come in a "set" with a mechanical pencil, which nobody other than technical drawers has ever used since 1812. Unless the recipient is actually a draftsperson, everybody else will take the mechanical pencil out of the box, break the lead within two seconds of trying it out, put it back in the box and never open the box again. Having a mechanical pencil in a set with a pen will actually diminish the value of the pen itself. On the other hand, any good (read "expensive") pen is an exceptional gift that the retiree will actually treasure – and make good use of. Tip – get the retiree's initials engraved somewhere on the pen for that personal touch. You're welcome.

4. Humorous Paraphernalia - A funny T-shirt, mug, ball cap or bobble-head is a really cute gift. From colleagues, they say, "Good luck pal – wanted you to know it's been fun having you around - your sense of humor will be missed." From a friend or family member, they say: "I want to acknowledge this important time in your life. We've shared a lot of laughs together - hope this makes you smile." A humorous T-shirt from the entire staff of a large office can only ever be presented as a much-appreciated bit of humor along with the "real" gift. If it is presented as the "real" gift, it can suggest to the retiree that their career has been a joke.

5. Gift Certificates – Even though a gift certificate is somewhat akin to giving cash and may hint that you lack imagination, giving one is rarely a faux pas. That said, do bear in mind that under no circumstances should it be redeemable at a grocery store (smacks of food stamps) or a pharmacy (just hurtful).

6. Artwork – By all means give a sculpture, a painting or a good print. The retiree will feel very appreciated. And there is tremendous comfort in knowing that, when all of the retiree's other earthly possessions have been divided up by the kids, sold or given to goodwill, the retiree will proudly display that artwork at the nursing home and fondly reminisce with everyone about their glory days at the office and how wonderful you all were. Of course flora and fauna are the safest choices, but for the right person, and you have to be absolutely certain that it is the right person, even a nude can be appreciated.

7. Rocking Chair - Both whimsical and practical, a rocking chair is an awesome retirement gift. Everybody loves rocking chairs. Even if there is no room in the house for it, the recipient will either throw out one of their old chairs or put the rocker on the porch. A rocking chair says that you have a sense of humor and you know that the retiree has one too. Giving a rocking chair doesn't say, "About time you retired, you old fogey," it says, "You've earned the right to put your feet up. Enjoy!"

8. Sports Equipment – From golf clubs to fishing rods, any piece of sports equipment special to the retiree says, "Thank you for you're service. You've been a sport." It also says, "We know you have plans for your retirement other than watching TV." The right piece of sports equipment will make the retiree feel valued and will be valued by the retiree. Good choice.

9. Kitchenware - There are a very select few retirees who either have dabbled or would like to dabble in gourmet cooking or baking. And anyone who has ever stepped inside a kitchen specialty shop knows that ninety percent of the items in that shop are well beyond the budgets of most working people, let alone those who are about to see a significant drop in disposable income. If your retiree is a budding chef, don't even think twice about what to get them. Whether it is a single Wusthof knife, All Clad saucepan, Le Creuset Saucier or Mauvier Gratin, the retiree will be thrilled, and you will be remembered as both generous and brilliant every time the retiree uses it. A clever gift for the right person, an appropriate kitchenware item says, "We understand your true passion and want you to enjoy the time you now have to indulge yourself." A word of caution: any gift of kitchenware to the wrong person says, "We've seen what you bring for lunch and, quite frankly, if you don't change your eating

habits we think you are going to die".
Well, Dear Diary, let's just hope the word spreads. Goodnight.

2. TIMING IS EVERYTHING

Sunday, February 7

Dear Diary:

Today is Sunday. As you will recall, I retired on Friday. Something has been nagging at me since yesterday, and I finally figured out what it is. This is the weekend. Everybody in the office has the weekend off. It doesn't seem fair that every single person in the office has had my first two days of retirement off. I feel robbed. No wonder I haven't felt any different. I've spent yesterday and today doing pretty much what I've done every other weekend for the past thirty years: laundry, grocery shopping and house cleaning. What a gyp.

Somebody should warn people not to retire on a Friday. If I could get a do-over I think I'd retire on a Tuesday. I'd set my clock radio that night for 7:00 a.m. just so I could wake up on Wednesday morning knowing I could hit the "snooze" button fifty times if I wanted. How sweet would that be - being reminded every seven minutes how great it is to be retired. ... Is that as petty as it sounds?

What the hell, tonight I'm going to set my alarm for 7:00 a.m. and tomorrow will be awesome!

Goodnight, Dear Diary.

3. DEUTSCHLAND, DEUTSCHLAND, UBER ALLES

Monday, February 8

Dear Diary:

Sadly, day three of retirement did not quite live up to my expectations.

Notwithstanding that I had given her ample notice of the impending change to our schedule, our one-year-old German Shepherd Dog, Lucy, is apparently unable to yet grasp that most fundamental principle of retirement known as "getting to sleep in". I am sixty years old. I have earned it. If I can't even sleep in when I want, what is the point of being retired? And I don't mean the Saturday, Sunday, Christmas kind of sleep in, I mean the calling into work "sick" on a Wednesday kind of sleep in.

Anyway, last night I went ahead with the plan to set my clock radio for 7:00 a.m. so I could enjoy hitting the snooze button as many times as I wanted. In hindsight, that was clearly a mistake. Despite my conversation with her about this very thing, apparently Lucy failed to understand the nuance in our little talk – the part where I said she was to ignore the radio alarm because Mommy was setting it just for "fun".

If you have ever owned a German Shepherd Dog you probably know what happens when the clock radio turns on in the morning. Whether you have it set to talk-show banter or classical music, it doesn't matter. A German Shepherd Dog always hears *Reveille*. It is the German Shepherd Dog equivalent of the Bat Signal. If their eyes are open, they are already at DEFCON 3. German Shepherds are working dogs. In fact, if you don't give them a job, they will make up their own (and quite possibly assume some of your duties. "Is that the teenager acting up again, Mom? Don't worry – I got this!")

I am reminded of this past Christmas when we had so many houseguests that I forgot to go out to pick up the poop in the yard for a couple of days (of course you know I mean the dog poop). You have to understand that every day of her life until then, Lucy had dutifully followed me around the yard as I scooped up her poop into bags for disposal. Each time I picked up a pile of poop I would say, "See what Lucy did? Good girl!" Never having owned a German

Shepherd Dog before, I was operating under the erroneous assumption that a relapse in potty training was an actual possibility.

You will appreciate then, how horrified I was, after only two days of forgetting to pick up, to notice Lucy in the yard with what appeared to be a frozen pile of poop in her mouth. I yanked open the patio doors and screamed. In her defense, she had previously only been trained for the command "Off," as opposed to the somewhat more complex command, "What the hell are you doing! If that's what I think it is, you are in big trouble missy!"

Completely ignoring my shriek, Lucy trotted up the stairs to the deck, opened her mouth and dropped her prize on top of what, to my alarm, was quite clearly a collection of other piles of frozen dog poop. There aren't many moments in life where the word "aghast" is the only word that can describe how you feel. I was aghast. But when she proudly looked over at me with her big toothy smile, I realized that what they say is true. If your dog is doing something weird it is not the dog's fault, it is the human's fault. And they are right.

When Lucy followed me around the yard picking up dog poop every day, she must have assumed that I was training her to do the same. So when I stopped doing the clean up, she took it upon herself to assume her new responsibilities. "Let's see. I don't have opposable thumbs, a scooper or a plastic bag – I know – I'll just use my mouth."

You could say that I learned two important things today; you only get one real first day of retirement, so make it a good one, and don't ever underestimate a German Shepherd Dog.

Goodnight, Dear Diary.

4. DECISIONS, DECISIONS

Tuesday, February 9

Dear Diary:

Having wisely chosen not to set my alarm last night, I slept until 9:00 a.m. Wow did that feel great! It is Tuesday, and I got to sleep in two hours longer than I have ever slept in on a Tuesday that wasn't a vacation day in the last forty years. The feeling was kind of like being on vacation only better, because there was just a hint of feeling smug.

But other than that, the only notable difference between being retired today and not being retired a mere four days ago, was that there was no real sense of urgency to anything. I had the time to just sit at the kitchen table and let my mind wander – aimlessly.

My first thought was that maybe I should finally organize the basement. Twenty years of living in the same house. Twenty years of uncurtailed impulse buying. Twenty years of, "Oh – that – just stick it in the basement." After reflecting briefly on the images burned into my brain from the last time I actually ventured down to the basement, I decided that organizing it was perhaps a bit ambitious for today. So I settled for pouring another bowl of Lucky Charms instead.

I'm not sure how I missed it all these years, but after reading the list of ingredients on the cereal box and confirming my suspicion that a bowl of Lucky Charms was maybe not the healthiest breakfast in the world, I started reading the other information on the back and discovered something amazing. Apparently, each tiny marshmallow charm is bestowed with a magical power. You heard me; those little rainbows, shooting stars, moons, hearts, clovers, hourglasses, horseshoes and balloons each have their own magical power. I seriously did not know that, and found myself devoting a not insignificant amount of time today to deciding which of the magical powers would be the best to possess. You see, unlike most fans of Lucky Charms, I am not a six-year-old who is content with the idea of having just any old magical power. Hardly. At sixty, I am much more discerning than that.

Some of the powers were relatively easy to dismiss. The power of speed, for example, was of no attraction from the outset, it having been many decades since I had felt the desire or need to "run" anywhere. I was also rather quickly able to determine that the power of luck was not the way to go, the precise nature of the luck being unspecified anywhere on the cereal box. I didn't spend thirty-five years practicing law for nothing. Finally, I think the Lucky Charms people should be informed that whoever dreamed up the power to "make things float" simply failed to fully appreciate the meaning of the word "power".

On the other hand, I have to confess that there was a certain amount of indecision when weighing the power to travel from place to place against the power of flight. I mean, I already have the power to travel from place to place if I can tolerate security checks and airline food… but what if it includes the power to "materialize" anywhere in the universe? And how does that compare to the power of flight, which would give me the opportunity to fly like a bird? These are not easy questions. And even if the ability to materialize anywhere was limited to just Earth, I could still "be in Rome" in the blink of an eye, which by anyone's standards is a pretty cool power (possibly with espionage applications, now that I think of it). If those were my only choices, it would have been a pretty tough call.

However, it was the final three options that were actually the most seductive: the power of invisibility, the power to bring things to life and the power to control time.

After some pretty serious thought I was finally able to eliminate invisibility as my choice for a power, because I figured it would only be of real value to a voyeur, a bank robber or a soldier. And as I didn't see myself realistically needing to engage in any of those activities for the foreseeable future, it came down to the final two. Would I want the power to bring things to life, or the power to control time?

You probably think that if I were a "good" person I would have chosen the power to bring things to life, but in the final analysis I wasn't satisfied that the power to bring things to life included the power to bring things "back" to life. Sure, I could conceivably blink a forest into existence where once there had only been desert, but what of the poor little squirrel who decided to run in front of my car at an inopportune moment? And wouldn't there be certain family members, friends and favorite pets that I might wish to raise from the dead? What kind of a lame-ass power is "bringing things to life" if I can't bring things "back" to life?

Therefore, I came to the only rational decision possible. I wanted the power to control time. Who hasn't fantasized about where they would go and what they would do with the power to control time. Of course I recognize that there is the potential for disaster – I've probably seen every TV show and movie ever created about time travel (like I'm alone). What with global warming, just as an example, how far into the future would you really dare to go? And as for the past, as cool as bringing a calculator and a lot of extra batteries to the Middle Ages or visiting Ancient Rome with a pocketful of disposable lighters might seem, I'm pretty much addicted to Tums, Hershey Bars, central heating and pizza. No, I would definitely limit myself to traveling back within my own lifetime. How great would it be to go back in time and buy Apple and gold stocks at the "right" times, or set off a few well-timed firecrackers from the grassy knoll? So, after hours (literally) of deliberation I finally concluded that yes, the power to control time was for sure the way to go.

My only regret about spending most of the day with a bowl of Lucky Charms? I just wish there had been a marshmallow for making things in your basement magically disappear.

Well, Dear Diary, it is time for bed. And, as luck would have it, I am still in my pajamas.

5. MALIGNANT GLAUCOMA

Wednesday, February 10

Dear Diary:

I had a medical appointment today. And, as difficult as this is to admit, I believe I may have learned something tiresome about myself.

Because I didn't have to rush back to the office after seeing the doctor, I spent the rest of the day on the Internet – and then the telephone. But here's the thing - when I described my latest medical issue to my friends and family I heard myself turning into one of those people that even I shy away from; you know, the ones who insist on lavish use of technical terminology with people who have absolutely zero interest in the subject matter.

I didn't say "I have a problem with the pressure in my eye." Oh no, that would be far too banal and, of course, fail to convey the uniqueness and urgency of my situation, or my level of medical expertise on the subject. I am (read "was") a professional, after all, not some simpleton who takes everything the "doctor" says at his word.

I had to tell everybody that I have "malignant glaucoma" and then go on in great detail about how the human eye works (which, by the way, is actually quite complex and rather fascinating – yikes – I don't seem to be able to stop myself).

But even that wasn't enough. Oh no. I had to go to even greater heights with those who hadn't yet made an excuse to get off the phone. "They performed an emergency iridotomy (explain), but I'm probably going to need a hyaloidectomy (explain), a core vitrectomy (explain), and possibly a goniosynechialysis (explain – add gory detail)." I let the words roll off my tongue like I hadn't just looked them up forty-five minutes before, like it was conceivable that in my spare time I had also become an ophthalmologist specializing in treating glaucoma. I could actually hear people rolling their eyes over the phone.

What is wrong with me? Am I that desperate for something "important" to talk about? "Sure, I don't have an interesting job anymore, but I do have malignant glaucoma – let me tell you all about that!"

There is no question that if I had discovered I had malignant glaucoma a year ago, it wouldn't have warranted much more than an occasional comment. I simply had too many other things to think and talk about.

But now that I'm retired, will I seize on every medical (and possibly dental) diagnosis or procedure to make myself feel like I am still relevant? Please let this just be a phase.

I have to go now, Dear Diary. But I feel like two Our Fathers and three Hail Marys may be in order.

6. RESPECT

Thursday, February 11

Dear Diary:

It's been less than a week, and already I am sensing a change in the relationship with my husband.

Several times a day now, Martin will "bump into" me in the kitchen or the living room and give me that look. His mouth says, "Hi Honey, what's up?" But his eyes say, "Oh. It's you. Are you still here?" I know the look well. It's the look I used to give my first husband after we had been married for less than a year.

I get it that things are a bit different for him now with me at home. He's always worked at home. Software engineers can do that. He gets up at 7:30 a.m. This is without, I might add, the benefit of an alarm. I don't know if it's simply being more in tune with Mother Earth than me, or pure sorcery. Either way, I find it incomprehensible (with a slight undercurrent of disconcerting).

Prior to my retirement, Martin would get up, shower and dress, make himself a double espresso and head up to his office. As I have been sleeping in since Tuesday, he now also has to let Lucy out in the yard and feed her before he can start work. I know. More work for him, even less work for me.

But it's not like I don't have things to do – I had that appointment just yesterday.

Anyway, I ignored "the look" for the tenth time today and then had to let Lucy in from the yard. Open patio door. Let dog in. Close patio door. Check, check and check. By my count, that's three jobs completed in less than five seconds.

Of course within ten minutes she was pacing and panting. She either sensed trouble in the air ("Mom! I think Timmy's fallen down the well!"), or had decided that I needed something to do, so she made it clear that she wanted back outside. Open patio door. Let dog out. Close patio door.

For some inexplicable reason (boredom?), when she asked to get back in again, I got it into my head that I'd try something new - really more to amuse myself than anything else. Back when I had a job last week, of course this thought would never even have crossed my mind. But you see, Lucy doesn't just sit at the door or bark when she wants in. She positions herself about a foot from the door and leaps up and throws her entire body against it over and over again until someone opens it. So, every five seconds you hear one hundred pounds of German Shepherd Dog being catapulted against the glass until she gets a response. Up until today, I would just open the door and let her in. That's right. Like a normal person.

But today I wondered to myself how she would react if, every time she leapt against the glass patio door, I did the same on my side of the door and yelled, "Let me out!"

I'm not sure what I expected her to do – it was kind of a spur-of-the-moment thing – but suffice it to say that by the time Martin intervened ("What is going on down here?"), I was exhausted and Lucy looked like she was high on crack or needed a dose of Ritalin.

And wherever I went for the rest of the day she was never more than six feet away with her unblinking eyes locked on me.

Dear Diary, I sense that Lucy may be losing respect for me.

7. NETFLIX: THE OPIATE OF THE MASSES

Friday, February 12

Dear Diary:

Well, Lucy appears to have concluded that it isn't necessary to keep me under observation any longer, so today I felt like I had the run of the house. But what to do. So many possibilities. So much time. So little initiative.

The truth is that I am just so tired that I really don't want to do anything. When I say I don't want to do anything, what I really mean is that I want to do nothing. Absolutely nothing. I am exhausted or, as my Father used to say, "exhaustipated" (fatigue-induced mental constipation).

In my working days I would have been up and showered, tended to Lucy, Twink (our fifteen-year-old cat) and Mr. Boogie (our twelve-year-old orange-cheeked waxbill), dressed, read the paper, done the Sudoku, the KEN-KEN, and the Crossword and consumed two cappuccinos by 8:00 a.m.

But by eleven o'clock this morning, all I had managed to do was get out of bed, throw on my bathrobe, make a cappuccino, look through the obituaries to confirm my suspicion that people my age were, in fact, dying and then wander over to the giant sofa in the living room and flop myself down in a fetal position.

A couple of hours later I woke up to the sounds of Martin making himself something to eat in the kitchen. "You feeling okay?" he called over his shoulder (polite-speak for "What the hell is wrong with you?"). "Yeah, just tired," I said (polite-speak for "Bite me."). We had developed polite-speak when the kids were small and never got out of the habit. But we both knew what we meant. Anyway, since it only takes maybe eight minutes to do it, I decided I probably should give Twink and Mr. Boogie fresh food and water and get dressed.

Surprisingly, those eight minutes of effort gave me a certain sense of accomplishment, so I decided that I had done enough for the day and went back downstairs to the sofa.

Because he is unable to tolerate commercial breaks on TV, Martin had signed us up for Netflix a while back. What an awesome invention. You get to watch the "good" commercial TV shows, but without the commercials. There should be a Nobel Prize for such things. Anyway, I scrolled around for a while and found one of my favorite old TV shows, *24*. That crazy Jack Bauer was forever getting himself into some sort of a fix that left you sitting on the edge of your seat until the next airing. So I clicked on Episode One of Season One. This was exactly what I needed.

When I woke up, Netflix was playing Episode Six of Season One, Jack Bauer was still in big trouble, and it was 5:00 p.m. I'm beginning to believe that it's no coincidence that the word "retired" can be used to mean "went to bed".

We ordered pizza for dinner.

Thank you for listening, Dear Diary.

8. PRACTICALLY ROMANTIC

Sunday, February 14

Dear Diary:

Well, today was Valentine's Day, and Martin and I celebrated the same way we have for the past twenty years or so.

All those years ago, having a new house to pay for and growing kids meant that a seventy-five dollar bouquet of flowers, expensive jewelry or lavish dining at a fine restaurant were all out of the question. And besides being expenses we really couldn't afford, they always struck both of us as way too cliché.

So, being the practical yet romantic people we both are, we came up with our own way to celebrate that was fun for both of us and didn't break the bank. Every February 14th we drive together to the local Dollar Tree, grab two carts and head off in different directions with twenty dollars to spend on Valentine treats for each other.

When we're done, we meet at the car and exchange the gifts one at a time until our bags are empty. Then we stop by the Dairy Queen for milkshakes before heading home for a spaghetti dinner (Martin's favorite).

It's nice to know that some things can remain the same - even in retirement.

Cheers, Dear Diary.

9. BEYOND THE PALE

Sunday, February 28

Dear Diary:

I know it has been some time since we have spoken. I didn't realize that there were one hundred and ninety-two episodes of *24* on Netflix. Needless to say, I haven't had a lot of time or energy for housework.

The funny thing is that I never used to have any problem fitting in a bit of housework when I had a fulltime job. I don't know why it should seem so overwhelming now that I am at home all the time. But as I looked around today – or, more technically, as Martin was showing me around today – I could see that someone hadn't exactly been "keeping up". While it was never really said that housekeeping is my job, I concede that it makes sense for the person who has the least to do (if you don't count watching *24*) to bear some responsibility for the more tiresome aspects of sustaining life.

However, it would appear that I have been in a downward spiral that revolves around sweatpants, Netflix and pizza. Even so, I was pretty insulted when Martin asked, "And when was the last time you showered?" Between you and me, if you saw the state of our shower, you probably wouldn't want to get in there either. On the plus side, I did save countless dollars in hot water bills, toiletries and cleaning supplies.

But the worst part of it all was that Martin had contacted my sister, Sarah, to be a part of what I now understand was an actual intervention. Apparently Sarah was also concerned because I never had the time to meet her for lunch or had anything to talk about on the phone other than Jack Bauer and the world of the Counter Terrorism Unit (CTU for those of us in the loop). Personally, I think Martin was just fed up with having to do the laundry and order in dinner and felt he needed backup. I mean seriously, after only three or four weeks of laundry and take-out he caves? How does he think I felt making dinner and doing laundry for the last twenty-five years?

Those considerations aside, Sarah and Martin decided to take matters into their own hands and, after tricking me into turning off the TV, they told me that they weren't going to enable me any longer.

To be perfectly honest, I was too tired to fight. I was also just a little bit uncertain whether they might seriously consider shipping me off to a rehabilitation facility if I didn't snap out of it. So I "admitted" that I had a problem. This appeased them to the point where they may even have felt a little guilty, because the next thing I knew, Martin went off to the grocery store and Sarah started furiously polishing the furniture and vacuuming the house. I took a long, hot shower and then started on the laundry.

Fortunately, the kids weren't around to witness my decline. Joey is still teaching English in Korea (the "good" Korea) – and to think I warned him that he'd never go anywhere with a B.A. in philosophy – and Grace is still married to that military fellow who keeps dragging her all over the world - they're living in Germany now.

It feels good to talk about what happened today. It really hurt my feelings. I'm not used to feeling like such a loser.

Goodnight, Dear Diary.

10. DIRTY JOBS

Thursday, March 3

Dear Diary:

I cleaned the bathrooms today then fell asleep on the couch.

I dreamed that Steve Jobs offered me a job. He said I could have any job I wanted. I said I would like to be his housekeeper.

The next thing I knew I was dreaming that I was paying for my meal at a deli and left my credit card sitting on the counter because I suddenly felt like I had to go to the bathroom. Thankfully, I woke up. The weird thing was that, after having a pee, I felt an overwhelming need to get back into the dream to make sure nobody stole my credit card.

Dreams. Who can say where they come from?

Goodnight, Dear Diary.

11. BLUE IN HAWAII

Saturday, March 5

Dear Diary:

I'm not exactly sure when it started, but I find myself turning immediately to the Obituaries column every morning when I read the newspaper. Unless something like World War III has erupted overnight, there is very little that distracts me from this fascination with the recently deceased.

The first thing I do is glance at the photos. Almost instantly I discount the ones who are clearly old. It's not that it doesn't matter to their families that they have passed on; it's just not all that unexpected (read "interesting"). What I am actually looking for is Obituaries written for pretty much anyone under seventy. I am sixty. I suspect that I am searching for confirmation that death is within reach. Our life expectancy is eighty-one for women and seventy-six for men. If you've managed to survive that long, then your death is not what anyone could call a tragedy, no matter how deeply your immediate family might feel your loss. And while accidental deaths hold a certain cachet all their own and do, therefore, pique my interest, they are not really what I am most interested in either. While they are true tragedies, they do not speak in any real terms to my deepest fears.

No, the Obituaries I tend to pour over are those announcing the deaths of forty to seventy year-olds. Which brings me to my point. It is super annoying when people don't mention the age of their dearly departed in the Obituary. We, your audience, sincerely want to know only two things: how old a person was when they died, and what killed them. Even if you give us a hint at the actual cause of death in the "donations appreciated" area, that will do. We have zero interest in the names of every single one of their nieces and nephews. We don't really care that they liked hiking (unless it was somehow related to their demise). We want to go through the daily Obituaries and find out how many people who could be us have died and of what.

"Let's see, today was five cancers, four heart problems and one Lou Gehrig's disease. And judging from the request for a donation to a mental health organization, very likely one suicide."

But those generalizations aside, and with sincerest sympathies to anyone who has had a loved one die in this manner, I feel compelled to tell you about one of the Obituaries I read in the paper this morning. Tragically, a middle-aged man lost his life in a snorkeling accident while on vacation in Hawaii.

I can honestly say that, until this morning, I would have been hard pressed to put the words "snorkeling" and "death" into the same sentence. Isn't snorkeling that thing where people look through masks at pretty fish in shallow water because it's easy and safe? Didn't I used to let the kids try out snorkels in the bathtub? Unless a shark came out of nowhere and grabbed him, I honestly couldn't fathom how a man could conceivably die from snorkeling. To tell you the truth, I was having difficulty imagining what a snorkeling "accident" could even be. It was as incomprehensible to me as if I had read that someone had tragically died as the result of a "hopscotch accident". I mean, seriously, how much trouble can a snorkeler get into? And even if he does, can he not just stand up?

This presented such a conundrum that I was seriously considering attending the man's funeral for no other reason than to find out what the hell actually happened.

"Please accept my most heartfelt sympathies. Poor Todd. So tragic, severing his aorta on a coral reef like that ... No? ... Becoming entangled in man-eating kelp?"

As there didn't seem to be any way of eliciting the necessary information without causing additional grief to Todd's survivors, I decided to turn to my most trusted expert on any matter, the Internet.

And to my utter disbelief, I discovered that snorkeling accidents are, in fact, the number one cause of tourist fatalities in Hawaii. Yes, you heard right, snorkeling is the single deadliest tourist activity in Hawaii. Am I the only person who did not know this?

If I had been asked just yesterday how I thought I could die while vacationing in Hawaii, "snorkeling accident" would not even have entered my head. I think we can all agree that shark attack would pretty much top everyone's list. Then, for the truly sporty among us, there is always the danger of succumbing to the bends while deep-sea diving, plunging a thousand feet to the ground while learning how to hang glide or getting hit in the head by a stray surfboard while frolicking in the water. There is also the ever-present threat of a small aircraft accident while island hopping (being an accident involving a small aircraft and not a small accident involving an aircraft). And of course, as with any seaside locale, you can never entirely discount the possibility of a deadly reaction to shellfish. Which is not to be confused with the not-as-rare-as-you-might-hope menace of falling victim to fatal food poisoning. In addition (although this may be a personal phobia), I would not exactly consider falling into a volcano in Hawaii to be beyond the realm of possibilities. Finally, what with Hawaii being technically a part of the United States, even a drive-by shooting might not come as a complete surprise. Yes, all of these would make my list. But snorkeling?

I mean if you decide you want to try skydiving, you understand that there are certain risks involved. You look over that Liability Waiver they hand you very carefully. And when you sign it, you do so with full consciousness of the seriousness of what you are about to undertake. But when you rent snorkels at a beachside hut from some guy wearing Maui Jim sunglasses and a necklace made of flowers, and he hands you a Liability Waiver to sign – let's be real – you treat it with about as much gravitas as you treat the "Not Responsible For Lost Articles" notice on your health club's locker-room door. It doesn't even register. "Sign where? Yeah. Whatever. Give it here." In fact, you probably just assume you are signing an agreement to bring back the snorkels.

I'm going to give you some free legal advice. Whenever you decide you want to "try" any activity, be sure to ask whoever is in charge, "Could I die doing this?" Be sure to ask it in front of witnesses.

So how is it that a person can die while snorkeling? Well, I read on to discover that the real problem with snorkeling lies with the strength of ocean tides and currents. Aha! Now that made sense to me.

You see the truth is, that I am no stranger to the power of the Pacific Ocean, having visited the California Coast in 1980. Try though I may to suppress the memory, I can still recall as if it was only yesterday those three terrifying seconds on a sunny afternoon at the ocean. I was standing in about two inches of surf waving at my girlfriends sunbathing on the beach when, with the kind of impact I would have assumed only an eighteen-wheel truck was capable of, I was suddenly driven by the water's force against my ankles face first into the salt and sand, where I was churned around like a ragdoll in a washing machine and then suddenly flipped back up on my feet facing in the opposite direction. Yes, I try to smile about it now (my girlfriends laughed hysterically at the time), but you don't soon forget such a close brush with eternity. Therefore, my heartfelt condolences go out to Todd's family with this cautionary tale.

And you can be assured, Dear Diary, that I will not rest until I have disseminated this information to all of my loved ones … and a few people I care about. Goodnight.

P.S. Scratch "Snorkeling in Hawaii" off bucket list.

12. TWINK

Thursday, March 10

Dear Diary:

I spent the better part of the day hanging out with our cat, Twink. I have to say that in the fifteen years she has lived with us, I haven't really spent a lot of "quality time" with her. She basically showed up at our door one morning and never left. She used to sleep with Grace at night, and now seems to spend most of the day lying in the sunny spot on Grace's bed.

When she noticed me standing in Grace's bedroom doorway this morning she rolled over on her back and stretched out her arms as if she wanted me to join her. So I lay down on the bed beside her and rubbed her stomach.

There is something hypnotic about a purring cat. And when I say "hypnotic", I don't mean "soothing". I mean a purring cat can literally hypnotize you, inducing a trance-like state and heightened susceptibility to suggestion. There can be no other explanation for how it was that I "awoke" several hours later in the middle of Grace's bed surrounded by cat toys and an open bag of Hairball Control Treats.

As if that wasn't sufficiently disquieting, when I was getting up to leave, I leaned over just to give Twink one last pat when, like a bolt of lightning out of the blue, I felt a sudden stabbing compression in my lower back that physically took my breath away and made me scream out loud. I couldn't move. Martin came racing into the room and grabbed me. I'm sure he thought I was having a heart attack.

I don't know what's worse - the excruciating pain - or the humiliation of having to tell people that I threw my back out petting a cat.

I miss Grace. Maybe she will get divorced and come home to me.

Goodnight, Dear Diary.

13. ARE THEY KIDDING?

Saturday, March 12

Dear Diary:

I spent all day yesterday in bed, taking Robaxacet and eating ice cream.

This morning I was finally able to hobble downstairs and make myself a cup of coffee and read the newspaper, and what I discovered has left me in a state of complete and utter disbelief.

Something is terribly, terribly amiss in the world of snorkeling. In an incident described as "never having been seen before", a young woman was killed today in yet another "snorkeling accident" – this time in Mexico. And it had nothing to do with ocean currents or tides. She was on a snorkeling tour boat when a whale breached the surface of the water and actually landed on the snorkelers.

Are you kidding me? It's starting to look like there's no way to not die if you go snorkeling. So, unless you are suicidal, or tired of seeing Great Aunt Mary suffer in her old age ("It will be fun. Just put this on. See the pretty fish?"), everybody everywhere should just stop snorkeling! It isn't worth it.

Goodnight, Dear Diary. I can't even think straight.

14. THE SOUND OF SILENCE

Wednesday, March 16

Dear Diary:

Throughout my working life it felt like I didn't ever have any spare time. I was never really sure what spare time would look like or be used for, because I never actually found any. But in my dreams, it was always that singular moment in time when I was not needed by anybody for anything. Not work, not family, not house, not pets. A blip in the space-time continuum. The antithesis of the perfect storm that was my life, spare time would be "the sound of silence". I had fantasies of waking up in the middle of Paris and discovering that I was the only person left on earth. How that was ever a premise for a horror story or nightmare I never understood. Not, at least, while I was still working.

But I am no longer working. That is actually an understatement. True, I am no longer employed, but the point is that I am no longer doing anything. I would go so far as to suggest that Twink gets more accomplished in a day than I do.

And I am starting to feel weird. It may have something to do with Martin having perfected his ability to ignore me while keeping an eye on me for the first hint of a Netflix relapse, but I don't really believe that. The truth is, Martin seems to be managing to cope with my omnipresence quite well. I suspect that the delivery last week of Bose noise-canceling headphones from Amazon.com has provided him with some level of assistance in that regard.

So I have been forced to face the fact that I feel weird for some reason other than Martin, and I have come to the conclusion that it has something to do with the perfect stillness of my life. I feel like the silence has descended. I am actually not needed by anyone for anything.

Okay, Mr. Boogie and Twink do still need me, but even if I really stretch out the feeding and watering and cage and litter cleaning, that only consumes about eight minutes of my day. There are one thousand, four hundred and forty minutes in a day. If I close my eyes when Martin comes into the room and never answer the phone, my life feels very much like I am the last survivor on earth.

But it is nothing like my fantasy, and not simply because suburban America lacks the cachet of Paris. What I feel is not the sense of peace and tranquility that I imagined. What I feel is a sense of nothingness, and it is not a good feeling. It is the stuff of nightmares and horror movies.

This must be why people have hobbies. I have never had any hobbies. I am not a joiner. And I have given Martin specific instructions that if he ever catches me gardening, he is to walk up quietly behind me and put a bullet in the back of my head. Just hearing the word "scrapbook" makes me want to stick an ice pick in my ear. I never joined a gym. I never took yoga, or its only slightly more annoying counterpart, "hot" yoga (although I have to confess to having tried a Netipot once which, by the way, produces a sensation that I am convinced is not entirely dissimilar to waterboarding and makes you feel like you are drowning yourself without the convenience of a bathtub).

Let's call it what it is. People have been making up crap to do to fill in the extra time they've had ever since they evolved from being hunter-gatherers about ten thousand years ago. The reason you don't see a lot of cave drawings depicting *Homo erectus* in spinning classes is probably because they were too busy just trying to survive. There was no spare time for fun distractions. For the 1.7 million years before we became agricultural societies and started domesticating animals, I imagine the conversation might have gone something like this:

"Hey Jmuk, see this rock I got in my hand?"

"Yeah."

"Well ... what if I throw it over to you?"

"Why?"

"... I'm not sure ... maybe you could catch it?"

"Why would I do that?"

"I don't really know."

"Why don't you just throw it at that reptile so we can have some food?"

But I get it. People don't do well when they have too much time on their hands. And if you examine the fundamental nature of most hobbies, it is clear that people don't actually undertake them to feel useful or productive (stamp collecting – need I say more). They simply have to have stuff to do that keeps them occupied before they go to sleep at night.

And that is precisely the problem with which I need to come to grips. How do I fill in my time? Because there does come a point (which, apparently, I have reached) where even Netflix, entertaining though it may be, simply doesn't cut it on a full-time basis.

So today I started making a list of all the things that I should or could do in a week. I am now dealing with a duty roster, if you will. While I may not actually "be" busy just yet, it seems that at least I have the potential to be busy. For today, that is close enough. The sound of silence has been disturbed.

Goodnight, Dear Diary.

15. *TEMPUS FUGIT*

Tuesday, March 22

Dear Diary:

Ever since retiring, I have relied on the Milk Calendar to let me know if there is anything pressing that I have to do on any given day. Generally speaking, unless it is somebody's birthday or I have a dental appointment, the calendar is pretty bare. As somebody once said, the trouble with having nothing to do is that you never know when you're done.

Of course I still refuse to press different numbers when I microwave anything, like there is any basis in reality for saving the precious millisecond it would take to press three-five instead of three-three, or one-two-zero instead of one-one-one. I'm way too busy for that.

But all of that "too much time on my hands" thing is about to change. I am so excited. I spent all day creating a weekly schedule. I am trying to be inspired by the fact that Easter is coming and I want everything to be nice. There are one hundred and sixty-eight hours in a week. I have set aside thirty-two hours for housework, seven hours for exercise, fifty-six hours for sleeping, ten hours for entertainment, fourteen hours for eating, ten and a half hours for personal grooming, five hours for visiting Mom and seven hours for walking Lucy. That leaves me twenty-six and a half hours a week for contingencies.

Notwithstanding the fact that none of the items in my new schedule would have warranted entry into my Agenda when I was working (example: 11:00 p.m. – read/sleep), I decided that from now on I am going to approach retirement like it is a profession. And, as every professional knows, effective time management cannot be accomplished without a Day Planner. I am a fan of hard copies of everything, and steadfastly cling to my suspicion that an electronic agenda is an accident waiting to happen (yes, I also refuse to give up my landline). So, I used up an hour and a half of my weekly personal grooming time in preparation for a mission to Walmart to acquire a new Day Planner.

You are probably wondering why I would need an hour and a

half of grooming just to go to Walmart. I love Walmart. I always have. I just never want to appear like I actually belong in Walmart when I go there. And so I dress up for the occasion. I don't mean "casual Friday" dress up; I mean black suit normally reserved for Board meetings dress up. I want anyone who might see me there to wholeheartedly believe that I found myself in Walmart purely by accident. "What? This is Walmart?"

As it turns out, my instinct to dress up for Walmart did not go unrewarded. Because, no sooner was I striding through the stationary section in search of my Day Planner than I ran into our neighbor, Charles Turner, in the Greeting Card aisle. FYI, Charles Turner has always liked to give people the impression that he was "to the manner (or in his case manor) born", if you know what I mean. More about Charles later, but suffice it to say that when we spotted each other we both, simultaneously, lost all power of speech and sense of coordination or direction, reminiscent of a pair of juvenile wild turkeys trying to cross a country road. I dropped my head and turned to my left, while stepping forward. He looked up at the ceiling, stuck out his right arm and took three steps backwards. Miraculously, we managed to extricate ourselves from the "situation". I grabbed the first Day Planner I saw and made a beeline for the cash register.

Under normal circumstances I would have done a little more shopping (since I was already there and had gone to so much effort to dress up), but the prospect of running into Charles for a second time was a price I was not willing to pay. The Charles Turners of the world are why I dress up when I go to Walmart.

Charles, on the other hand, was not as nattily dressed as I would have expected. Except, of course, for the "good" shoes. He always wears such "good" (read seven hundred dollar cordovan leather) shoes. But there was something amiss about his overall attire – no, can't quite place it. But it will come to me.

As usual, Lucy greeted me at the door when I got home. Lucy is not comfortable when one of her charges is out of her sight, and seems compelled to provide a full report of all goings on during any absence, even if it has only been for twenty minutes. Of course I interpret all her changes in tone and inflection as a rather extensive vocabulary:

"Oh Mommy. I didn't know where you were. Is that another

dog I smell on you? Somebody walked across our driveway while you were gone. And Daddy made a sandwich and didn't give me any. And Mr. Boogie gave himself a bath in his water dish and splashed water all over his cage. And then there was a loud noise across the street. And also the cat wouldn't let me upstairs to see Daddy. Then I heard the toilet flush. Then I saw a squirrel run across the back deck. I was a good girl. I didn't let any burglars in. Do I get a cookie now?"

I really wished I had spent more time at Walmart. It felt so good to be wearing a suit again that I didn't want to take it off. But, according to my schedule, it was time to prepare dinner, and I had defrosted some Italian sausages.

You have to understand, it is only recently that I have come to realize that the freezer is an actual food storage tool; that it can be used as something other than a mere way station for the garbage bin. For my entire working life, the freezer was just the place where ice was made and food went before it got thrown out, sort of like limbo for leftovers.

Now that I have the time, we go to Costco and buy twice as much meat as we can eat in a month and, when we get it home, I wrap each piece in individual "portions" bags and put them in labeled freezer bags for future defrosting and cooking. It's really quite ingenious. Wish I had thought of it twenty years ago.

Anyhoo, after preparing dinner, eating and cleaning up (which consumed one and one half hours of housework time and three quarters of one hour of eating time), there were two hours allotted for "entertainment" (read "Netflix") before my 11:00 p.m. read/sleep deadline.

Whew, *tempus fugit*, Dear Diary. Goodnight.

16. ORBIT CITY

Thursday, March 24

Dear Diary:

Our son Joseph was visiting our daughter Grace (and her husband) in Germany this week to celebrate Grace's birthday, so they thought it would be a good idea to Skype Mom and Dad.

Why can't people be satisfied with a nice phone call anymore? I like the phone call. In fact, I was planning to call her anyway, like a normal Mom does on her daughter's birthday. The trouble with Skype? People tend to sound a whole lot better than they look. And of course they all have retina display on their computers, so every line and age spot is crystal clear. It wouldn't even be quite so bad if I could pretend for my own sake that I looked sensible, but no, not only do they have to see how disheveled I am, I get to see myself looking like "John's other wife" throughout the entire conversation.

Am I the only one who thinks that Skypeing people is tantamount to dropping by their house unannounced? I don't want you to be able to look in on me at any time of the day or night. I don't want to look in on you, either. I don't want to watch you eating your dinner, folding your laundry or brushing your cat's teeth.

I can remember seeing George Jetson's videophone when I was a kid and thinking, "Who would want people to see them every time they answer the phone?" I was seven. Mind you, I had a lot of time for the dial-a-meal, but even as a child I recognized that the videophone was creepy.

Can we all just agree that whoever invented Skype should be drawn and quartered? Every time the kids call they want to talk on Skype. If I can't go to Walmart without getting dressed up, just imagine how I feel about somebody seeing me in a ratty bathrobe with no makeup on, sitting in the middle of the kitchen where last night's dishes are strewn across the counter. I'm at an age where I can't just throw myself together on a moment's notice. Give me a break!

And while I'm on the subject of communications in general, have you tried to make contact with anyone under thirty by telephone or email recently? Don't bother. Send them a text, on the other hand, and you get an instant reply. Can you hear me now? A prediction: in one hundred years people will all have double-jointed thumbs and have lost the ability to speak.

Sorry about all that, Dear Diary.

P.S. The kids were fine. But Grace doesn't appear to be contemplating divorce. We wished her a Happy Birthday anyway. Goodnight.

17. HIPPITY-HOPPITY

Monday, March 28

Dear Diary:

They're gone! Finally! It would have been different if either of the kids had been able to come home for Easter, but with just Martin's folks, my Mom and us, Easter dinner felt more like punishment than anything else. It's one thing when the kids are here to lighten the mood or change the conversation, but the five of us alone for two days is really more than I can stand.

To start with, the fact that both Mom and the in-laws live just close enough that they expect to be invited for holiday celebrations is compounded by the fact that they all live just far enough away that they have to stay overnight.

And of course Mom doesn't drive. Dad, rest his soul, put an end to that the day she asked him if it would "hurt the car to drive it without gas". He was a saint. She lives one and a half hours away, so we also have to make sure we don't arrive back here without absolutely everything she might need or want for forty-eight hours.

Never having been encumbered by ownership of a driver's license herself, Mom doesn't seem to appreciate the fact that it might not be convenient for us to take three hours to retrieve her favorite slippers she forgot at home. "Well I don't understand what the problem is, I'll just watch the television until you get back." Yikes.

Add to that the fact that - well, it isn't just one fact, there's a list:

1. They all have hearing aids. Not one of them ever wears their hearing aids. For a week after they leave, Martin and I are still talking to each other as if we're cast members in a performance of *Don Giovanni* at the Met.

2. Aksel and Camilla expect leg of lamb to be served at Easter dinner. Mom thinks "Easter isn't Easter" without a big, baked ham. I have one oven.

3. The first course at the dinner table is never food. It is a series of pills that must be taken with food. Invariably, someone has forgotten or lost their pills. Our friend the doctor is contacted. Favors are traded. The food gets cold or dried out while a pill run is made.

4. Camilla brings her special beets and turnips dish to serve with dinner. Mom claims it gives her gas.

5. Mom expects me to make "her" scalloped sweet potatoes with hazelnuts and corn fritter casserole. Aksel will need to use his Epipen if he eats a hazelnut, and Camilla suffers terrible indigestion if she eats corn.

6. I can't run the risk of complimenting Camilla within earshot of my mother.

7. All weekend long, no matter where he is sitting, within about five minutes Aksel always says the same thing, "Is there a draft in here?"

8. Aksel and Camilla have a long-standing tradition. They speak with one voice. That voice is Aksel's. My mother has a long-standing penchant for bringing up controversial subjects that provide her with the opportunity to exercise her not inconsiderable debating skills. I believe the technical term is "shit disturber". Aksel and my mother do not get along.

9. Camilla drinks. Camilla is addicted to The Shopping Channel. We are all under strict instructions to take the telephone away from her if she picks it up.

10. If he catches your eye, Aksel will launch into a long-winded story he has read in *Reader's Digest*. He will always forget the ending. Or the point. The only other thing he is interested in discussing is the weather. From the moment they arrive until the minute they leave, he is either looking out the window, presumably for an impending weather emergency, or asking each of us if we have heard what the weather is going to be for tomorrow.

11. I've never been able to figure out which one of them it is, but either Camilla or Aksel snores so loudly that the rest of us have to wear earplugs whenever they visit. My mother swears it is Camilla.

Fine. They're old. They know what they know, they like what they like and they do what they do. But they all appear to have turned into caricatures of their former selves, with every weird aspect of their personalities becoming more exaggerated with each passing year. I spent the entire two days feeling like a contestant on *Survivor* who wanted to be voted off the island.

There were only two activities that brought any semblance of tranquility or happiness to the holiday; yesterday Martin took them on a long drive to show them the sights while I prepared dinner, and this afternoon we served them lunch in front of the giant screen T.V. to watch *Singin' in the Rain*. That's right, not wildly dissimilar to babysitting a group of three-year-olds for the weekend.

Okay. Now that I have that off my chest, I guess I should also mention that we really do love our parents. Aksel is the one who taught Martin how to fix everything. My Mom is probably the reason I was able to handle a job where virtually every interaction was adversarial. And Camilla? Well, Camilla is just very sweet - and her Shopping Channel jewelry really is kind of pretty.

They've all gone home. We're glad they're gone…but we're also glad they're "still around".

Goodnight, Dear Diary.

18. CASH FOR TRASH

Wednesday, March 30

Dear Diary:

Martin is a wonderful husband. Martin is also a hoarder. Fortunately, his hoarding is confined to items that get stored in the basement and the garage, so at least we don't have to fight our way past stacks of old newspapers, bric-a-brac and dead cats to use the toilet. As you know, he is actually quite persnickety when it comes to the rest of the house (that's right, the part for which I am responsible).

At this stage in my life I don't really care about the junk in the basement any more, but I still cling to the hope that some day I will be able to use a small space in our over-sized double garage for my car. And every once in a while (usually when it is raining or snowing outside) I will mention this to Martin.

However, things just seem to keep getting worse. Not only is there no room in the garage for my small car, I bought a bicycle last summer and had to store it on the front verandah all winter because Martin couldn't find room for it in the garage. It is difficult for me to understand how, in a space that is twenty-five feet by thirty-five feet (I have lived in apartments that were smaller than that), there is no room for a bicycle. Couldn't he even hang it from the rafters? Well, apparently not.

But if I put an empty glass, metal or plastic container in the recycling bin instead of hiding it in a garbage bag, he will retrieve it and "set it aside" for an imaginary future use. Make no mistake about it, space will miraculously open up in the garage if an empty plastic dog cookie barrel or coffee tin is at risk of becoming homeless.

And while most people who replace an old, stained and chipped bathroom countertop might set it out at the curb on garbage day, Martin is not most people. That countertop (which, by the way, is actually bigger than my bicycle) has been in our garage for the past five years. Martin's explanation to me when I found it taking up space in the garage? "It'll give me a flat surface to work on."

I have one bicycle. Martin owns every model of every make of every tool that a professional contractor would need to run a business. There is so much stuff in our garage that I can't even find the garbage bins any more. I just open the door and blindly throw the bags of garbage in and cross my fingers that they will find their way to the curb by Monday.

In light of all of that, you can imagine how startled I was this morning when I glanced over at the bulletin board in our kitchen and saw a new note tacked up. It was in Martin's handwriting, and it said "Cash For Trash" with a phone number underneath and the words "will call back". I almost burst into tears of joy. Could it be true? Had twenty years of snide remarks finally paid off? Was Martin finally going to do something about the garage?

I felt like I had misjudged him, and fondly recalled our second date when he showed up at my apartment door just after I had dropped an earring down the bathroom sink. He didn't have a bouquet of flowers with him that night, but by God he did have a plumber's wrench in the trunk of his car. I sure didn't have any complaints about his tools then, did I?

I was so thrilled with what I assumed could be nothing other than evidence that he had finally decided clear out the garage, that I made him a Nespresso and took it up to his office - just to show a little appreciation (and make absolutely sure I wasn't hallucinating).

All smiles, I knocked on the door and poked my head in. He lifted up one side of his noise-cancelling headphones.

"Hey. What's up?"

"Thought you might be ready for another coffee."

"Great. Thanks."

"...so?"

"What?"

"I see you've decided to get rid of some of the junk in the garage."

With his head tilted to one side like a dog searching for the meaning of my words, he said, "What junk?"

It wasn't just the words that made my heart sink; it was the utter sincerity with which he said them. And although the words and the cocked head were not good signs, and I had every reason to believe the conversation was headed in a bad direction, I couldn't stop myself from pressing forward.

"...I saw the note ... Cash For Trash?"

The knot between his eyebrows signaled an unsettling failure to recognize any connection whatsoever between a business called "Cash For Trash" and a garage full of junk.

"Cash For Trash?" I repeated, hoping that maybe he just hadn't heard what I had said (but knowing with absolute certainty that he had).

"Oh, that... Yeah... I'm looking for some used parts for the old lawnmower Dad gave me last year."

I was so stunned that I couldn't speak. My husband, the hoarder, had placed a call to a business that goes by the name "Cash For Trash" ... not to unload any of his trash ... but to try to buy some of their trash.

Clearly pleased with himself for being able to address the issue with which I had interrupted him, he smiled and dropped the headphone back onto his ear. "Thanks for the coffee."

There were only three possible options left for me: murder Martin, kill myself or just walk away.

I had been planning to vacuum the entire house today. I watched Netflix for fourteen hours instead. It is now 12:40 a.m. and I am going to bed, Dear Diary. Goodnight.

19. THE LYRICS PARADIGM

Monday, April 4

Dear Diary:

The project I gave myself for today was to memorize the words to *The History of Everything*, the theme song created in 2007 for *The Big Bang Theory* by the band Barenaked Ladies (who are brilliant).

Not as easy a task as you might think. After listening to it about twenty times I finally had most of the words down pat, but I still couldn't seem to get what comes between "The earth began to cool" and "We built a wall, we built the pyramids".

It's a great song – very catchy – but there were those sixteen pesky syllables that were completely incomprehensible to me. I couldn't stand not knowing what they were saying. All I heard was:

"be ba bo bo be ba boo boo
be ba ber ba be beh buh boo"

With sufficient confidence that Martin wouldn't know what I was up to (noise-cancelling headphones), I replayed the song somewhere in the neighborhood of one hundred and thirty-seven times. Still nothing. So I caved and looked it up on the Internet. FYI, the incomprehensible lyrics are actually:

"The autotrophs began to drool,
Neanderthals developed tools"

That's right, "autotrophs". I'm guessing that out of a world population of approximately seven billion people there are maybe a dozen (thirteen, if you include me) who know what an autotroph is. And I only know what it is because I can't stand not knowing what a word means so I had to look it up (an organism that takes energy from the environment in the form of sunlight or inorganic chemicals and uses it to create energy-rich molecules such as carbohydrates).

Now, I ask you, where was the Internet when we were all trying to figure out the words to *Louie Louie*?

I need some sleep, Dear Diary. Goodnight.

20. THE "RETURNS" COUNTER

Tuesday, April 12

Dear Diary:

I know it's been a while since we've chatted, but on the bright side, I finally found a hobby. It's called "shopping", and it's really quite a lot of fun.

I've forgotten all about trying to keep up with a housekeeping schedule and there is still a lot of frozen meat in our freezer, but I am actually starting to enjoy retirement.

It all began innocently enough – grocery store, pharmacy, Walmart, but then my sister, Sarah, took me under her wing. And not a moment too soon. After the Cash For Trash fiasco with Martin, I was perilously close to acquiring a deep-fat fryer and knocking us both off with my cooking. It was sort of a long-range murder-suicide plan. Fortunately, it never came to that.

The only drawback to taking up shopping with Sarah as a hobby is that - how do I put this delicately – we're just not in the same financial league. When we first started going shopping together, she would buy a cartful of stuff everywhere we went, while I would wander around filling up my cart, but then just leave it in an aisle when it was time to go. I know it sounds a bit pathetic, but make no mistake, even that gave me a certain amount of satisfaction.

Predictably, however, the time came when I was no longer happy to simply abandon my cart full of great buys when our shopping trip was over. I started slowly, choosing one or two items to buy on each shopping trip. Now, had we confined our expeditions to once a week or so, everything probably would have been okay. But Sarah is an inveterate shopper and, as her newly deputized assistant, I was on duty at least three or four times a week.

Before too long, and you probably saw this coming, I was shopping with such abandon that there was no more picking through my basket for my favorite one or two items. I was marching up to the cash register with the full cart – every time. And when I got home, I didn't even take all of the stuff out of the bags anymore. I just kept piling bags in my closet, one on top of the other. On the plus side, I was racking up Aeroplan miles like there was no tomorrow. It wasn't just a shopping spree, it was a shopping frenzy. And although I didn't really need encouragement, Sarah was always there to offer it. "That's gorgeous! You can't not get that!"

Boy we had fun ... until Martin ruined everything by blindsiding me one day with the Visa bill. I felt like a four-year-old who had been caught licking the icing off all the cupcakes. Was it as humiliating as the Netflix disaster? Not quite. But close. Very, very close. The shame was on the same level, but ever so slightly easier to take in the afterglow of conspicuous consumption. At least I had "something to show" for my behavior; or, as Martin put it, "something to return".

So, as dutifully as I had followed her to the cash registers, Sarah came with me to the Returns counters. Which was where we discovered that not all retail outlets have the same Returns Policy. Apparently, some establishments strictly impose a limited number of days during which you are entitled to return an item for a full refund, after which they only offer a store credit. Well, my Visa bill being what it was, a store credit simply wouldn't do.

While Sarah had been my mentor on the "buying" side of things, she was sadly lacking as far as the "returns" end of the shopping experience went. In fact, it's probably not an exaggeration to suggest that Sarah had never even considered the option of returning anything in her life. "People do that? It seems like such a bother." Let's just say that it's worth your while to drop into Goodwill if you are a size eight with really good taste and happen to be passing through our town.

So, here's the thing. If I think something isn't fair, I am not "like" a dog with a bone; I am a dog with a bone. It doesn't matter how big, how loud, how smart, how rich or how powerful you are, you will never intimidate me. I am the Black Knight in *Monty Python and the Holy Grail*. Needless to say, any retail "situation" is mere child's play.

How, you may ask, does that translate when dealing with a clerk at the Returns counter advising me as sweetly as possible, "Oh, gosh. Yeah. Sorry, but that is our store policy." (Emphasis on "is" as if the policy had come down from Mount Sinai chiseled on a stone tablet). Tip number one: Don't be afraid of awkward silences. If none exist, create them. An awkward silence is to a human being what a virus is to a computer. Every human being on earth is preprogrammed to crash when faced with an awkward silence. And when a person runs out of words to fill the void (and if you do it right, they will), that person will enlist the assistance of another human being. Always. That other human being will ultimately be "the manager".

"The manager" is the person you really wanted to deal with all along. But (and this is tip number two) never, ever, under any circumstances whatsoever, ask to see the manager. If you ask to see the manager, raise your voice, insult the staff or create any kind of a scene, you have already lost. You are not there to beat anyone down or "win". The only reason you are there is to return an item for a refund. You should never be perceived as a threat or a problem. You should remain benign. Better that the staff think you are a little simple than think you are a troublemaker. Besides, if you do ask to see the manager, you are likely to get the following response, "I'm sorry, the manager's not in right now." Then, you are reduced to asking for "whoever is in charge," and it just goes downhill from there. The whole idea is to have the clerk come to the conclusion that the only person who can rescue him or her from you is the store manager.

And this is how you do it:

"Yes, ma'am. Can I help you?"

"Yes, thank you. I'd like to return this." Be polite, calm and expressionless.

"Do you have the receipt?"

"Yes." Hand over the receipt. Keep it simple. No flare.

"Oh. I see you bought this seventeen days ago." Ignore this comment.

"But I can give you a store credit."

"No, thank you. I would like a refund." Be polite, calm and expressionless.

"I'm sorry, ma'am, but you only have fourteen days to return items for a full refund. You bought this item seventeen days ago. I can give you a store credit for the full amount."

"No thank you. I would like a refund." Be polite, calm and expressionless.

"Oh, gosh. Yeah. Sorry, but that is our store policy."

"No thank you. I would like a refund." Be polite, calm and expressionless.

"I'm sorry, ma'am. That won't be possible." Smile politely. Do not say a word.

Allow the awkward silence to work for you. If a lineup starts to form behind you, ignore it. That lineup will actually work to your benefit, because it will start to unnerve the clerk at the Returns desk.

Eventually, the clerk will either say, "Excuse me for just a moment," which means they are going to ask their supervisor what to do with you, or they will give it one last shot and say, "Do you understand what I'm saying?" to which you will reply politely, calmly and without facial expression: "Yes, thank you. I'd like to return this."

Repeat this exact tactic with every staff member up to and including the manager. The difference, of course, is that for the manager, the "store policy" is merely a guideline. The manager always has the discretion to be reasonable. If you have your receipt, you are clearly not trying to put anything over on the store. Store managers understand risk assessment. Giving you a refund presents no risk. On the other hand, while you have been nothing but polite, you remain an unknown (and possibly "odd") quantity, and a steadfast refusal to give you a refund has the potential to go any number of ways, most of them not good.

So stay the course, and whether the manager is a smartly dressed young woman, a gruff looking, overweight middle-aged man wearing a tie or a nineteen-year-old with a nose ring and a full sleeve tattoo, the awkward silence you have so politely created will eventually be broken by the manger signaling to the clerk to just give you the refund.

Say, "Thank you," as if the refund was always understood.

Sarah was so taken with the whole concept and the fool-proof methodology, that by the third day of hitting Returns counters she was bringing along some of her own stuff just to try it out. "Oh my God, this is so easy. It's like making money!"

She's not entirely wrong. And it makes you wonder whether or not there are any real limits to what you can "return"... I understand the local football franchise may be up for grabs...

Goodnight, Dear Diary.

21. *SIDDHARTHA* REVISITED (Herman Hesse, 1972)

Wednesday, April 20

Dear Diary:

For the first time in a long time, I found myself searching our bookshelves today for something to read. And I came across a book that I haven't even thought about since 1972, Herman Hesse's *Siddhartha*.

Just picking it up made me smile. I curled up in our oversized armchair and reminisced about university days; hip-hugging bellbottom jeans that scraped the floor so the hems would purposely fray, tie-dyed T-shirts, peasant blouses, homemade love beads and anything with fringes on it.

We were young, and we smelled of tiger balm and patchouli oil. We talked about Watergate and Vietnam, and we knew what astrological sign all our friends were born under. With "Peace" signs dangling from leather strips around our necks, we hitchhiked everywhere. We soaked our water buffalo sandals in water so they would form to our feet and we chastised our parents for using pink toilet paper. With our bodies wrapped around each other on the tiny dance floors of smoke-filled campus pubs, we listened to *Knights in White Satin*, *Wild Horses* and *Stairway to Heaven* blaring from quadraphonic speakers. We burned incense and we burned bras.

When our parents became curious about the giant "TOKE" posters on our walls, we just told them it was the name of a new band. We scoffed at the military-industrial complex, joined sit-ins and dangled tiny brass bells on colored strings from our door handles. 1972 was the year of *Deliverance*, *Everything You Always Wanted to Know About Sex (but were afraid to ask)* and *The Godfather*. We read *Fear and Loathing in Las Vegas* and *Rolling Stone*, and everybody had their own copies of *Jonathan Livingston Seagull* and wanted *Watership Down* for Christmas.

I put on a T. Rex CD, closed my eyes and thought about the Zen teachings that had so inspired my youthful heart. Even suffering is part of the great cyclical unity of nature. Every being carries in it the potential for its opposite. We must love the world in its completeness. **Follow your own path.** Time is just an illusion. We must strive to find enlightenment.

The phone rang. It was Sarah. "Want to go return some stuff?"

"All mine has already been returned."

"Don't worry. I got lots."

"...You don't have any weed, do you?"

Dear Diary, we didn't do any "returns" today, but we had a really, really, really great time. I love Sarah. I love you. Goodnight.

22. EXTRA! EXTRA!

Saturday, April 23

Dear Diary:

Just when I thought my usefulness to society was at an end, I discovered that our local newspaper is searching for people with valid drivers' licenses and reliable vehicles who want to earn up to twelve hundred dollars per month working only three hours per day.

    I mentioned it to Martin. He pretended he didn't hear me.

    He may change his tune when it comes time to pay the Visa bill ... I'm just saying.

    Goodnight, Dear Diary.

23. TO DREAM OR NOT TO DREAM

Tuesday, April 26

Dear Diary:

Last night Martin had one of his episodes where he becomes quite animated and talks in his sleep. Technically, it's called REM Sleep Disorder, but Martin claims he's simply trying to get a word in edgewise.

    I awoke to find him sitting bolt upright in bed with the duvet pushed down to our feet. Eyes wide open and darting back and forth, he was staring intently at the sheet like a hunter on the prowl. And every few seconds he would stab at something imaginary on the bed with his finger and yell "Aha!"

    This was something completely new. Usually, these events involve loud, animated discussions about politics (in which I sometimes participate just for the hell of it). So I watched him for about three minutes, trying to figure out what on earth was going on in his head.

    Finally, I couldn't stand it any longer and said, "What are you doing, honey?"

    "I have to get them."

    "Get what?"

    "The robot bugs."

    Puzzle solved. "You're having a dream, honey."

    "Okay."

    Who knows what tomorrow night will bring. But I have to say that the entertainment value alone is often worth the sleep disturbance.

    Goodnight, Dear Diary.

24. WHAT DID YOU SAY?

Friday, April 29

Dear Diary:

I have always taken pride in the fact that I look youngish for my age.

When I was in my late fifties, I was on my way to the Vancouver airport in a taxi when I suddenly became very ill (complicated migraine with aphasia). I felt like any movement would produce projectile vomiting, I was perspiring heavily and I couldn't move or speak. When the taxi driver saw what was going on and that I was unable to respond, he pulled over and called an ambulance. When I get these spells, even though I am in a terrible physical state and probably appear not fully conscious, I am actually totally aware of everything that is going on around me. I could hear the taxi driver describing my symptoms to the 9-1-1 operator. And then I heard him say, "I don't know ... maybe forty?"

This probably says more about me than anyone should know, but without a word of a lie, as close to death as my body felt, and as impossible as it would have been for me to physically smile at the time, my brain still went "Schwing! He thinks I look forty!" We take our compliments where and when we find them.

So, bearing that in mind, you can imagine how stunned I was this afternoon when the cashier at the hardware store, after ringing up the new plunger and toilet seat I had bought (don't even ask), looked me straight in the eye, all smiles, and said, "Do you qualify for our seniors' discount, ma'am?"

I'm guessing everybody remembers the first time they are asked that question. Nobody goes around saying, "Oh gosh, I can hardly wait. In three months I get the seniors' discount." I have never been in a line-up at a store and overheard anybody saying to a cashier, "Excuse me, but I just turned sixty today. Do I get a discount?"

I felt like you could have heard a pin drop; that the entire hardware store had fallen silent. She might as well have asked me, "Would you like a frontal lobotomy with that today?"

This twenty-year-old Pollyanna had found my Achilles' heel (she should work at the Returns counter). Notwithstanding the fact that I actually did not want her to repeat herself (or provide me with more information about the seniors' discount), I heard myself saying, "What did you say?" I knew the moment I said it that it was a mistake.

Not being a mind reader, she replied, "Everyone over sixty gets twenty percent off their purchase on the last Friday of every month." Note to self: Do not leave the house on the last Friday of any month.

Clearly, everyone in the store agreed that I looked sixty. Which is to say that no one gave any indication that they were as shocked by her question as I was. Well, it would appear that the only way my brain could deal with the situation was to come up with some way to convince everybody in the store that I did look young for my age. There's no other way to explain what I said next: "Yes I do qualify. I'm actually seventy-two."

I could see from the looks on everyone's faces that indeed they did think I looked very young (for seventy-two). And, as pathetic a testament to my fragile ego as the entire exchange may have been, I chalked it up to a "win", picked up my parcel with the vigor of a sixty-year-old and strode lithely out to my car.

But on the way home I thought about it some more. To tell you the truth, I haven't stopped thinking about it. Why is it that men under sixty don't give a crap about looking young for their age? In fact, if you tell a twenty-two-year-old man that he looks young for his age, he may be insulted. Men want to look seasoned, mature and experienced. But tell a twenty-two-year-old woman that she looks young for her age, and she will spend the rest of the day admiring herself in the mirror. "I do look young. I could get carded."

The truth is very simple. When people don't actually know you, they will judge a man by what he does, and a woman by how she looks. However, the people who do know you will use entirely different criteria, none of which have anything to do with what you do or what you look like. They will judge you on the kind of person you are, and they are the ones who really matter.

So I've come to a couple of conclusions. First, I can never be twenty-five again. Let's face it, I can never be fifty again. I am sixty years old. It wasn't always easy getting here and, quite frankly, I should be proud that I made it this far. An awful lot of people in this world never do. Second, to a person in their twenties, everybody over forty looks like a senior citizen. That is a simple fact. The cashier had not intended to insult me. She probably would have asked the same question to someone a decade younger than me and not realized that she was hurting their feelings.

So if somebody wants to give me a discount on the cost of something because I am sixty years old, then I think I will choose to take that as a compliment from now on and resolve to go boldly into senior citizenship with pride, knowing that how old I am has nothing to do with who I am.

And if your establishment doesn't offer me a seniors' discount, I may just decide to take my business elsewhere.

Just trying to keep it real, Dear Diary. Goodnight.

25. THERE IS A GOD

Monday, May 2

Dear Diary:

Wow! Things are not what they used to be! Not around our neighborhood, anyway. I think I told you some time ago about running into my neighbor, Charles Turner, at Walmart. In the kerfuffle that ensued I recall vaguely registering that there was something "wrong" about Charles' appearance, but couldn't quite put my finger on it.

Well, I've got my finger on it now. And when I think back, I realize that what must have thrown me off at the time was that Charles just naturally radiates such smugness and superiority that my brain interpreted the blue vest he was wearing at the time as simply a poor clothing choice rather than the obvious. You see, Charles has now got a part-time job at Walmart. Or as he would no doubt put it, "taken a temporary assignment in retail".

As you well know, I am the first person to understand the desire or need to either keep yourself occupied or earn a little extra cash in retirement. Let's face it, I wasn't one hundred percent kidding when I pointed out to Martin that there was an opportunity for me to get a paper route.

Not that Charles could qualify as being retired, because in order to be retired, you have to have been doing something in the first place. So unless you count "living the good life" as an occupation, Charles is not a retiree. He is an employed senior.

For the twenty years we have lived on this street, Charles Turner has always given us the impression that we are merely being tolerated; that we don't quite qualify to be in his presence. I believe it's a British aristocracy thing. All his real friends seem to have titles like "Lord", "Lady", "Sir" or "Baron", and there isn't one of them who doesn't have a double-barreled surname. "When we were last on Lord and Lady Flippety-Floppingsworth's yacht..." You see, in his mind people are actually not born equal, "One man, one vote you say? Nonsense. Utter nonsense."

To give you some idea of how his personality played out in the "hood", while we sometimes had to keep a car going with duct tape and prayers, he has always driven an impeccably maintained British Racing Green vintage Jaguar with tan leather interior. Charles and Daphne (his wife) don't invite the neighbors to barbeques; they invite us to garden parties. When our kids were blaring electric guitars in our basements, his were thumping out *A Maiden's Prayer* on a Grand piano in their salon. And Charles Turner's standard response to almost any comment you might make is, "Yes. Quite," which is the British version of "Uh huh."

When we were budgeting for new IKEA bedroom furniture and window blinds, Charles and Daphne were painstakingly overseeing the reupholstering of their Chippendale window chair and carefully ensuring that their hand made Rubelli custom drapery textile perfectly complimented their Louis XIV commode. I think you get the picture.

So you can see why it's probably safe to assume that Charles would not be huddled with the masses at Walmart for charitable reasons or kicks. No, there can be only one reason, and it has to be financial disaster of some form or other. Either the trust fund took a nosedive or the castle fell to ruins, but there is no doubt that our Charles is short of cash. And I'm pretty certain that Walmart was the only place where he could get a job because, up until now, Charles has never worked a day in his life.

There is a God.

You must think I'm being mean. Well, I suppose I am, a bit. It's just somehow uplifting to see a person like Charles finally get a bit of a comeuppance. I don't want the man to suffer, but maybe it will do him some good to get a taste of what the rest of us have been going through our whole lives while he has been languishing on his verandah sipping gin and tonic.

If you don't count my personal run-in with Charles at Walmart, I officially learned of his new status from my neighbor, Sophie. Unlike me, when Sophie came across Charles at Walmart, she immediately took note of the blue vest and nametag and strode up to him and said, "Hello Charles, are you working here now?" To which, she says, Charles replied (apparently without skipping a beat), "How are you, Sophie. It is so lovely to see you, my dear. You will excuse me, but I simply must be off."

Of course being the super-friendly, kind and still innocent person that she is, Sophie suggested that perhaps it would be less embarrassing if we all simply pretend not to see Charles if we ever encounter him at Walmart.

I might have gone another way with this information but, as you know, not being one to readily admit even frequenting Walmart, I could find no flaw in her reasoning.

But there is a God.

Goodnight, Dear Diary.

26. JOEY, JOEY, BO BOEY

Wednesday, May 4

Dear Diary:

Well, today was Joey's birthday. And, while a small part of me thinks children should send their mothers presents on the day they gave life to them, Martin and I stuck with tradition and mailed Joey a card wishing him a Happy Birthday and sent him the gift he always asks for - an INTERAC e-Transfer of money. He is his mother's son.

Thank goodness my Mom doesn't travel. There is very likely a thrift shop in Seoul featuring every holiday sweater, pair of cufflinks, patterned polyester shirt and calculator she has ever sent him. He may have kept the socks.

Yes, twenty-three years ago today our eight-pound boy slid into the world. Even the doctors had never seen a baby weight exactly eight pounds. There's always at least one ounce. Not Joey. Everything about Joey has always been precise. Even his personality. Very balanced. He always seemed to know who he was, what he wanted and how to behave. He never had to be told anything twice. He was never foolish.

His plan is to spend three years in South Korea teaching English as a second language while taking a Master's Degree in Oriental Philosophy at Seoul National University. He will save money, gain international experience and become fluent in another language. He has one year left, so he has written the LSAT and applied to Law School. Not Law Schools, mind you, Law School. Harvard. That's just the kind of kid he is. His plan is to graduate from Harvard Law School.

Martin and I have learned to just accept the fact that, for now at least, Joey is not a "Plan B" kind of guy. And so we have ceased offering practical advice like, "Don't you think it would be a good idea to at least apply to other schools…you know…in case you don't get accepted at Harvard?" We figure that life will blindside him soon enough in one way or another, and that will be the point at which he learns that nobody has quite as much control over what happens to them as they might like to think they do. We all learn that lesson eventually. Joey will too. And he will be okay.

For the time being, we are content to let him have his dreams and make his plans.

Happy Birthday, Joey.

Goodnight, Dear Diary.

27. AND NOW THE SHIPPING NEWS

Friday, May 6

Dear Diary:

Did you know that you can buy almost anything online and have it delivered to your front door for free? It's true. And it's addictive.

It doesn't matter that we have access to every kind of retail outlet imaginable within about a ten-minute drive, once I discovered that I didn't even have to leave the kitchen table to acquire precisely the same items, it almost seemed ridiculous to contemplate doing anything else.

And it's like the online retailers know me. I can be looking up a medical condition totally unrelated to shopping, and a J. Crew ad will pop up and show me some adorable new jeans that I have actually been looking for – and they will be on sale. I know! It's amazing!

Just today I ordered roll-on deodorant online and got a free lip balm thrown in. Mind you, I had to order enough deodorant to last for thirteen years to qualify for free shipping, but so what?

I love free shipping. In fact, the UPS guy and I are starting to become quite friendly.

The Internet – why would you shop anywhere else?

Well, Dear Diary, I'm off to take a warm bath and then wrap myself up in my new cashmere robe from overstock.com.

Goodnight.

28. SUDDEN-ONSET ASS EXPANSION

Tuesday, May 10

Dear Diary:

I have spent my entire (unpregnant) adult life at exactly the same weight and wearing exactly the same size of clothing. Until now.

It seems that overnight I have gained twenty pounds. You would think that I might have noticed it at maybe five or ten pounds – but apparently not. No, without warning of any kind, I have gained precisely twenty pounds. And it would appear that twenty pounds is the dividing line between size eight and size ten. You can still get away with wearing your size eight clothes if you gain twelve or seventeen pounds, but not twenty. I know this because I have been fitting (albeit somewhat snugly) into my size eight clothes up until this morning.

This morning, I could no longer do up my size eight jeans. I don't mean that I had to hold my breath to get them on (that was last week). I mean I couldn't get them up past my ass.

I could understand all of this if I had been an exercise nut who had suddenly stopped working out, or if I had taken to dropping by the Dairy Queen for a medium chocolate milkshake every day for the past two and a half months, but I haven't changed anything. I have never exercised, and I only hit the D.Q. maybe once a month – same as always.

So, why the weight gain? Because that's what it is, despite the fact that I briefly considered the alternative - that I had contracted a new medical condition defined largely by "sudden-onset ass expansion". But even when I looked it up in Latin, *repente impetus incrementum asinum* is apparently not a symptom of any recognized disease. Which leaves me to conclude that running around all day at the office and stressing about my case load all night when I was a working person, must have actually used up calories. I know it wasn't like real exercise, but I guess at least I had the benefit of being in motion all day.

Diet and exercise. Diet and exercise. We have all heard the advice. Everywhere you turn you hear the same pat phrase. And, as reluctant as I generally tend to be to jump onto any bandwagon, this morning my jeans strongly recommended that perhaps I should reconsider that position. "Whoa! Whoa! What is she thinking? We're never going to fit over that ass!"

But as I've never really been an over-eater, I don't believe that diet is where the problem lies. The truth is, ever since retiring, I have probably gotten less exercise than Twink.

So I decided it was time to consider buying myself a treadmill. I mean really, how hard could it be?

I have to say that it surprised (read "hurt") me a little that there wasn't even a moment's hesitation or protest from Martin. I had half expected at least one "Really? You look fine to me," but when it wasn't forthcoming I accepted that as a sign that a treadmill was in my immediate future. In fact, Martin wanted us to go over to Costco right away and get one.

And that is precisely what we did. But here's the weird thing. I thought that after Martin and Tony (Sophie's son) set it up, I would just turn it on and "go for a run" like I see them doing on TV all the time. Almost everybody appears on a treadmill at some point or other, and they even carry on conversations while they run - like it's perfectly natural.

For the uninitiated, I am here to tell you that if the most exercise you have ever done in your life is to stretch your arm out to grab your bag of food from the drive-thru window, you cannot just hop on a treadmill and "go". I know, because I tried it. Within ninety seconds I was out of breath and the room was starting to spin.

If you had asked me yesterday what kind of shape I was in, I would have said "okay". That would have been a lie. I am not in "okay" shape. I am in horrible shape. That is not to say that I have a horrible shape. While twenty pounds heavier than normal, the actual shape of my body is just fine. And for my entire life I had assumed that if my shape was fine, I was in good shape. No. As it turns out, those are two entirely different things. So I am now resigned to getting into shape, and it looks like it will be an uphill battle.

After recovering from my dizzy spell, I did a ten-minute walk at a moderate speed. Who knows, maybe some day I'll be able to do a forty-minute walk on a five-degree incline, but I won't be overdoing anything just yet.

Goodnight, Dear Diary.

29. FILL 'ER UP

Thursday, May 12

Dear Diary:

It struck me when I got gas (for the car) today, that half the people at the pumps were senior citizens. And I think I know why.

Getting gas is actually an agenda item for retirees. "Think I'll go and gas up the car, dear. Care to join me?" Retirees never run out of gas. True statement. Pun not intended.

Nobody else on the planet gets into their car and sets out for the sole purpose of getting gas. For most people, getting gas is an annoying task, not an event. That's why they fit it in on their way to or from somewhere else, somewhere important. But retired people leave their house just to get gas and then go home. "Can never be too careful. Don't want to run out of gas when I go to the dentist next week."

Getting gas is actually a social outing for a retiree. In fact, I think gas outlets would do well to take that into consideration when they plan their stations. Have one row of pumps set up with comfortable little stools beside them. This is not a fleeting moment in a retiree's otherwise hectic day. This is their day. Make it special.

Standing while you pump gas is like eating your breakfast over the kitchen sink. Make your filling station like a *Cheers* set for seniors. Have speakers installed and make better use of all that information you're collecting anyway about your customers. Just imagine how much a retiree would enjoy frequenting your filling station if, while seated on a nice cushioned stool as they are pumping gas into their vehicle, they heard over the sound system, "Good morning, John. How are you doing today? Can I get you anything else? A diet Sprite? A box of Kleenex, perhaps? Have a good day."

C'mon, software engineers, there ought to be an "app." for that!

Just a thought, Dear Diary. Goodnight.

30. BZZZZ

Sunday, May 15

Dear Diary:

Something is happening to my brain. I used to do the puzzles in the newspaper every morning before going to the office. Out of habit, I have continued doing them ever since I retired - but with one significant difference. While it used to be that I could finish the entire crossword in about fifteen minutes, it can now take fifteen minutes just to figure out one clue.

I appear to have lost the ability to concentrate on anything more difficult than a review of the items in my online shopping cart.

It occurs to me that I probably spent fifty-five of the last sixty years exercising my brain. Tell me it's not ironic that the moment I decide to start exercising my body, my brain gets flabby.

What the hell, maybe I'm okay with that. It's not like the Supreme Court is waiting with baited breath for my brilliant legal insights. It's not like Western civilization will collapse if "the Chinese" finish the crossword puzzle before I do. I don't even need to make sure I get the correct change at the grocery store any more. Martin and I aren't going to be homeless if I don't write a best-selling murder mystery. And let's face it, I've already figured out which marshmallow Lucky Charm has the best magical power. Maybe my work is done.

Sarah called this afternoon. She was blabbing about how many hornets she had caught in her hornet trap on the back patio. What she couldn't understand was why there weren't any in the trap on her front porch. "Yeah. That is weird," I volunteered. I didn't have the guts to tell her that when we were over at her house for dinner last night I set the hornets on the front porch free. I just couldn't stand to see them struggling desperately to keep from drowning in the sweet liquid they were trapped in.

Don't get me wrong. I'll smash a hornet with my shoe in a heartbeat. It was the prolonged suffering that seemed unnecessarily cruel. I know. I'm the crazy one.

It's just that ever since the bumblebee incident a few years back, I feel less inclined to harm most insects. Earwigs and mosquitoes are the only exceptions. Trust me, after you realize that you've killed a firefly by mistake and had to watch its tiny glow fade to nothing, you won't even kill a fly again. Just in case. As for earwigs and mosquitoes, I don't even use a paper towel any more. My fingers do just fine. But bumblebees? I have a pact with God that I will never hurt another bumblebee again in my life.

The whole thing started when I was spraying primer on a couple of spots on my old car. After sanding all the areas around the wheel wells, I had just begun spraying when a big, fat, slow bumblebee started buzzing around me. It wouldn't leave me alone, no matter how often I tried to whisk it in another direction with my arm.

Finally, half out of fear of being stung and half out of pure frustration, I aimed the can of primer at him and sprayed. In hindsight, it was clear that my assumption that spray primer would act in much the same way as a can of Raid, killing him instantly, hadn't been well thought out.

What followed was so horrible that I find it difficult to think about even now. The bumblebee did not die instantly. Soaked in a blinding, smothering coating of light grey primer, he fell to the ground, writhing around the grass and making a weird, low buzzing sound that still haunts me. I tried to step on him to put him out of his misery, but the grass was just long enough that every time I tried to squish him with my shoe he was somehow cushioned by the grass between the sole of my shoe and the ground.

Desperate to put an end to it all, I ran into the garage to find something heavy enough that it would penetrate the grass and kill him. All I could find was the axe. I raced outside brandishing the axe and, blunt side down, smashed at the convulsing tiny body in the grass over and over again until the buzzing finally stopped.

It all seems so surreal now. I have never forgiven myself for ending his life that way. He should have died of old age in a field of clover with a last sip of nectar lingering in his mouth. No bumblebee deserves to die blinded and smothered by automobile primer and being crushed to death by an axe.

I've never been able to take the word "overkill" lightly since. I hate myself.

Goodnight, Dear Diary.

31. VALHALLALAND

Wednesday, May 18

Dear Diary:

I had another nightmare about pirates last night. I don't know where my fear stems from, but pirates absolutely terrify me. Maybe it's because they have always been portrayed as ugly and mean, smelling of rotting fish and with eye patches, peg legs or hooks for hands. And in my recurring nightmare, the ugliest and meanest pirates around have captured me.

What I am actually doing "on the high seas" in the first place is anybody's guess, but I am frightened out of my wits as I am being forced to walk a gangplank suspended over dark, stormy waters. Yes, I wake up before I fall overboard, but always in a cold sweat.

Pirates are not to be confused, however, with Vikings, with whom I have had a great sense of affinity ever since I watched a video of *The Vikings*, starring Kirk Douglas. I can guarantee you that every little girl who ever saw *The Vikings* has spent the rest of her life fantasizing about being swept away by a Viking. Vikings are strong, handsome and fearless.

But other than "Pirates bad / Vikings good", I think somebody should do men a favor and let them in on what we women really do and don't want in our men. So I spent some time thinking about it, and came up with a few tips.

What Women Don't Want: (Note: If you have any one of the attributes on this list it is going to be extremely difficult for you to find and hold onto a woman without using chloroform and cable ties.)

1. Sensitive: When your girlfriend or wife says you are "sensitive", she is not complimenting you. She doesn't really want you to be so perceptive that you immediately detect and respond to her every nuanced look or gesture. Women don't want you to always be trying to guess what they are thinking and feeling. They're not always sure themselves what they are thinking and feeling. Give them some breathing room. If they have something on their minds, trust me, you will hear about it. In real words. This does not,

however, give you license to be an ass.

2. Clever: Not to be confused with "smart", a "clever" man is wildly unappealing. You can know what the phrase *bon mot* means, but if you ever use it in a conversation, you are history.

3. Well-Groomed: All any real man ever has to be is clean. If you spend time in front of a mirror for anything other than shaving, you might as well fold up your traps and go home.

4. Well-Dressed: Wearing nice clothing is not the same as being "well-dressed". Forget the "little touches" that elevate your outfit to "well-dressed" status. And the only acceptable remark you can ever make about your own attire is, "Is this okay, honey?" which pleases her because it indicates that you've never spent any time figuring out what "goes" with what or how to "accessorize". Two thumbs up!

5. Well-Mannered: You don't need to behave like you were raised by wolves. You can and should be polite. However, there is a fine line between being polite and being obsequious. The second you cross over into sycophant territory you will lose her. If people are commenting on how "well-mannered" you are, you have crossed the line. Your manners should never be so good that you appear unctuous. Nobody likes a toady.

6. Dramatic: There is only room in a relationship for one person to be dramatic. That person cannot be the man.

7. Angry: Anger is perhaps the most disturbing of the emotions, and any display of anger is a sign of weakness. A woman counts on her man to be both predictable and in control, of himself if nothing else. How can you take care of her if you are weak? How can she rely on you if your behavior is unpredictable? She can't. Chances are good that any man who has ever been described as having a "hair trigger" or a "tricky" personality, has also been described as "single", if not "incarcerated". Although I hesitate to give you this information, there actually is one very narrow exception to this rule. You are permitted (read "encouraged") to briefly display smoldering (never overt) anger if any other man flirts with your woman.

8. Bejeweled: There are only five pieces of acceptable jewelry on a man. Your Dad's ring, your wedding ring, your engineering ring, your university ring and a watch. A word of caution: Under no circumstances are they all to be worn at the same time. The only exception to the "five" rule is for those of you who are of Latin

descent and wear an inconspicuous religious icon around your neck. Okay, there is one more exception. A Super Bowl ring. Okay, okay, a MedicAlert bracelet is wearable, but remember that it does signal a level of physical weakness that you may not wish to advertise to prospective mates.

 9. Romantic: Unless you are dating a twelve-year-old (which will probably ensure that you spend the rest of your life in a place where the only time you will even see a real woman is on visiting day), forget about rose petals, candlelight, bubble baths, bouquets of flowers and big public gestures. That is all soap opera bullshit. None of it is "hot". A woman wants you to show her how hot you think she is. So meet her at a secluded motel, take her on the kitchen counter or press the "Stop" button the next time the two of you are alone on an elevator. Get it?

What Women Want: (Note: If you have all of these attributes, then you don't need this list. For the rest of you, if you can get a total of five points out of nine, you will have absolutely no problem finding a woman who will be proud to be your partner.)

 1. Strong: If you have testosterone coursing through your blood, then you are already stronger than almost every woman alive. So chalk up one point just for that. See how easy it is? Women don't need or want you to spend twenty hours a week pumping iron. They want you to be able to lift the forty-pound bag of dog food into the grocery cart, build a deck off the back of the house and operate the snow blower. Even if you are in a wheelchair, when you put your arms around her she needs to feel your strength. It makes her feel safe.

 2. Calm: You must be her rock. Throughout her whole life she is going to be experiencing hormonal fluctuations, from PMS to pregnancy and menopause. She will be emotional. She can't be calm. She needs you to be. Hint: If just reading the words PMS, pregnancy and menopause makes you nervous, you do not get a point.

 3. Literate: You don't have to be a University Professor, but the first time you say "supposebly" will be the last time you see her.

4. Funny: We don't want you to be the life of every party or a stand-up comedian, but you do have to recognize humor and appreciate it. A good sense of humor is very sexy. The Three Stooges or Red Skelton - not so funny. John Oliver, Louis C.K., Larry David, Bill Murray and Bob Newhart - comedy geniuses.

5. Generous: This has nothing to do with money. Don't go racking up a giant Visa bill so you can impress her. She will hate the monthly payments much more than she will enjoy the fancy restaurants. If you have the money to be generous in a financial way, then that's fine. But it is not the point. It is generosity of spirit that really tells her what kind of a man you are. Want to really impress her? Then offer to spend a Saturday afternoon helping your aging Mom get her groceries. Anyone with cash can throw cash at a situation. But when you are generous with your personal time, you are in a whole other league. And she will take note.

6. Circumspect: Be prudent in what you say and do. Don't jump to conclusions about anything or anybody. Make it clear that you think things through before making decisions. She doesn't want to feel like you have dragged her out onto thin ice. Ever. Note: If you had to look up the meaning of this word you are probably not relationship material. Please deduct one point. Also note: If you have ever lost money in the stock market, please deduct one point. Just kidding! We all lose money in the stock market. 2008. Who knew? And not losing money in the stock market doesn't make you circumspect, it actually strongly suggests insider trading so ... if you have never lost money in the stock market please deduct one point.

7. Fearless: Think brave. Think courageous. Think intrepid. Think Viking. The most important element of fearlessness is self-confidence. Note: Any activity undertaken while under the influence of alcohol doesn't count. Things only "seem" brave when you are drunk. If you have ever been in the military, add two points.

8. Ambitious: You don't need to be the CEO of a Fortune 500 company. You don't necessarily even need to be gainfully employed. With the world economy being what it is today, plenty of highly eligible men (and women) will quit or lose their jobs at least once during their adult life. What is critical, however, is that you possess a skill, trade, talent or profession that can translate into a source of income and enough self-respect to pursue that end. If you have ever started your own business, give yourself an extra point.

9. Handy: If you can tick off this item, then you get three points. Not joking. You may even get away with saying "supposebly" once or twice. If you can change the oil in her car, hang a light fixture without starting an electrical fire, install a kitchen faucet or a new dishwasher without having to "call in a professional", then you, sir, are worth your weight in gold. There isn't a woman alive whose heart doesn't flutter just a little bit when she sees her man using a power tool. If you hold a hammer like a girl, deduct two points.

You may have noticed two glaring omissions from this list of What Women Want. They are "handsome" and "rich". First, "handsome" is entirely subjective. Every woman has her own idea of what "handsome" is. Second, and contrary to popular belief, "rich" is irrelevant to ninety-nine percent of women.

As for the one percent for whom "rich" is relevant, well, they actually aren't even called women. They are called something else.

And on that note, Dear Diary, I will say goodnight.

32. THE SWORD OF DAMOCLES

Friday, May 20

Dear Diary:

I had my annual gynecologist visit this morning. Stupid. I had made the appointment back when I was still working; not even thinking about the fact that I would be retired by the time it came up. I had to be there for 8:00 a.m. Stupid. You spend your whole working life fighting to get early morning appointments, and then when you retire, all of a sudden the thought of having to be somewhere for eight o'clock in the morning is enough to make you apoplectic. Of course in order to be there for 8:00 a.m., I actually had to get up at 6:00 a.m. Stupid.

Working people are living in a forest of daily activities. Retired people are living in a desert. For a working person, an appointment is just another tree in the forest. But for a retired person, an appointment takes on the proportions of a giant Redwood in the middle of an otherwise flat, barren landscape.

When a retired person flips the page on the Milk Calendar and sees there is an appointment scheduled in the upcoming month, they immediately check to see if the appointment is for them or their spouse. There is a tremendous sense of relief if the appointment belongs to the spouse, "Oh honey, remember you have that dentist appointment on the 18th." But if the appointment is for them, there is no end to the emotional turmoil that will plague them for the entire time leading up to it. They will not be able to "do" anything for seventeen days:

"I was going to start exercising today, but I see I have that appointment coming up in a few weeks."

"I wanted to invite the MacMillans over – maybe I better wait until after my appointment."

When you're working, you just fit your appointment in on the way to the rest of your day. Kind of like stopping at a gas station. But when you're retired, "the appointment" hangs over you like the Sword of Damocles for weeks in advance.

Which is why, as appointment day approaches, we will try our damndest to come up with an excuse for cancelling:

"It's just a limp. Maybe it'll go away on its own."
"Do I really need to get my teeth cleaned every year?"
"It's not like I have a hair emergency."
"Yup. Looks like it might rain next week."

You know those times when your doctor says he will put you on a cancellation list? Get on that list. Chances are very good that a retiree has a scheduled appointment that will be cancelled. Why do you think they even have cancellation lists? It's not because normal people cancel appointments willy-nilly. Normal people don't cancel appointments unless they are in a car accident on the way to an appointment.

It's retirees. We only ever make it to fifty percent of our appointments. We will even cancel surgery bookings. Yes, those appointments that take up to six months to get? We will cancel at the last minute. It's not that we're worried about the surgery, we're just not sure we will feel like getting up, showering, dressing, driving and parking our cars on that day.

Of course the longer you are retired, the more adept you become at appointment making. It doesn't matter if it is for a blood test, an MRI, a periodontist, a manicurist or a veterinarian. Eventually, every appointment we make will be based on only two criteria: location and time. We don't care how good you are at what you do; we only care where you are located and whether or not you have an opening at a "good" time.

Retirees want all their appointments to be between 10:30 a.m. and 2:30 p.m. You see, an appointment before 10:30 a.m. may require us to get up that day at a time when we might not feel like getting up. That's impossible to predict in advance. And don't expect us to drive in rush hour. That's not going to happen. We will pull over and go to a restaurant until rush hour (and our appointment) is over.

But, if you give us an appointment at a "good" time and we don't cancel in advance, we will never be late. You can count on us retirees to not hold up the line. In fact, we'll probably show up about twenty minutes early. It's what we do.

That's it for tonight, Dear Diary.

33. GUERRILLA GARDENING

Monday, May 23

Dear Diary:

With the minor exception of the year we had to tell him that his rose bed bore too much of a resemblance to a burial plot, my Dad was an amazing gardener. He was the one with the green thumb.

Our yard and our house were filled with beautiful, thriving, flowering plants. He spent countless hours designing beds, digging, preparing the soil, planting, fertilizing, watering, mulching, pruning and weeding. It was his passion, and the results spoke for themselves.

He even built a little garden shed that had windows and tables and a sink with running water. It was filled with all the gardening paraphernalia you could imagine; small tools, large tools, a wagon, a wheelbarrow, bags of mulch and fertilizer, soil and river stone, special gardening gloves and aprons, watering cans, transplanting pots of every size, nature and kind, and even gardening books.

He approached gardening like a military operation. His planning spanned months and years. He could envisage exactly how everything would grow and develop and how to optimize each site according to sun exposure, drainage and wind direction, constantly marshaling the forces of nature to his advantage. He was in it for the long haul. Nothing was left to chance. Our garden was the envy of our entire neighborhood. A real estate agent would have said that our house had that elusive "curb appeal".

But, much as I appreciated the results of all my Dad's efforts, I never caught the gardening bug. Even after I was married to Martin and we moved into our lovely home, I just never had the time, the inclination or the talent to recreate the wonderful outdoor spaces my Dad had built for us.

While it is arguable that I now have the time, my approach to gardening has always been low-intensity and much less phase-driven.

My equipment consists solely of a dozen or so ceramic planters strategically placed near seating and viewing areas that more give "the impression" of a garden than actually qualify as a garden.

There are no tools; there is no uniform. There are no gardening gloves or bags of potting soil, mulch or river stone. There are no daylong excursions to pick up the latest botany intelligence at gardening centers.

I start in May making small raids on grocery store displays as I am approaching the cash register and pick up one of anything that has flowers on it. Buying one at a time allows me to escape with as few casualties as possible.

By the time the end of May comes around I have enough plastic pots of flowers to fill all my decorative planters. If they are in plastic hanging planters I use a pair of scissors to cut off the "hanging" parts and dump the pot into one of my nice planters.

There is absolutely no maintenance provided to these plants over the entire summer. They are watered by the rain or they die.

In October I throw the remains in yard waste bags.

I spent twenty minutes today doing my "gardening". Whew! Goodnight, Dear Diary.

34. HOLD THE ONIONS

Sunday, May 29

Dear Diary:

I had only one item on my schedule for today, and that was "take a shower".

I remember the days when showering was a semi-conscious morning ritual undertaken between letting the dog out and getting dressed. There was no thought to it; never any question about "whether or not" to shower. It was like brushing your teeth.

Not so much since I retired. The first thing to go was the whole concept of the "daily" shower. Quite honestly, unless you are very sweaty, work out every day or spend time hanging out with smokers, even employed people don't really need a daily shower. They do it simply out of habit or an abundance of caution.

These are the kinds of things you have the time to think about when you are retired from the hamster wheel of life. And I have concluded that showering is a choice.

But be warned, once you have crossed the "showers are optional" threshold, there is no end to the variables to be taken into consideration. Do you shower every second day as a matter of course? Do you shower on an "as needed" basis? Do you shower once a week (whether you need it or not)? Do you live in California where water consumption is an actual issue? Do you live in Seattle where rain could conceivably serve as a shower substitute in the warmer months? Will you be leaving the house? Do you have a medical appointment or are you just going to the grocery store? Will you be taking your coat and/or footwear off? Will you be wearing anything sleeveless? How good is your deodorant? Did you eat onions since your last shower? Will anyone be taking your photograph? Will you be required to give a speech? Do you own a bidet?

I don't mean to lead you astray. There will be circumstances in which showering is not optional. But, in my humble opinion, those circumstances are actually quite limited:

1. You want to have or recently have had sexual intercourse (with another person);

2. You have an appointment that will involve close physical contact with a professional with whom you expect to have an ongoing relationship (not to be confused with #1);

3. You are attending or hosting a gathering of family or friends (exception: pool party);

4. You have exercised (strenuously);

5. You have vomited or had diarrhea;

6. Other people are saying you have body odor;

7. You have eaten onions or been in an enclosed space where onions were being cooked or

8. It is Sunday night and you haven't had any other reason to shower all week

It's probably obvious from the list above that, if you can avoid onions, the average retiree only needs to shower on Sunday nights.

Well, Dear Diary, tomorrow is Monday, and the start of a new week.

Good night.

35. MIRROR, MIRROR

Wednesday, June 1

Dear Diary:

When Sarah and I were at T.J. Maxx today we saw a small mirror with 20X magnification.

Of course we both laughed, "Who would want to see themselves 20X magnified?" (You know, at our ages.)

But I have to tell you, what I was really thinking was, "Who wouldn't want to see themselves 20X magnified?"

So, as we were wandering around looking at other stuff, I kept trying to find a surreptitious way to head back to the beauty supplies aisle and slip the mirror into my basket without Sarah seeing.

While it's true that it might not be for the faint of heart, I could think of at least a zillion uses for a 20X magnification mirror. Eyebrow plucking. Applying mascara. Finding that bristly chin hair you can feel the tip of before it gets long enough for anyone to actually see. Blackheads. Nose hair. Age spot alert. Post spinach dental examination. Those tiny, hardened clogged pores you can't attack without creating a carbuncle in the middle of your face (like I'm the only one who's ever done that).

Applying eyeliner. Applying lip liner. One micron off on either one of those procedures and you can end up looking like Bette Davis in *Whatever Happened to Baby Jane.*

I didn't just want the 20X magnification mirror; I needed it.

I finally "got separated" from Sarah in the shoes section (she's a seven and a half, I'm a ten) and made a beeline for the beauty products.

But as I rounded the corner to the aisle, who should I see fondling the very 20X magnification mirror I was after, but Sarah:

"Hey...Have they got another one of those?"

"Oh. Hi. I started thinking about it, and..."

"I know. Me too."

"Eyelash stuck in your eye."

"Moustache bleaching."

"This thing is awesome."

"Oh good. They have two."

It's great having a sister like Sarah.
Goodnight, Dear Diary.

36. LIFE WITHOUT PAROLE

Monday, June 6

Dear Diary:

It's hard to believe, but thirty-five years ago today, Martin and I exchanged our wedding vows in St. Patrick's Basilica. What was I thinking?

Actually, I know exactly what I was thinking. I was thinking how lucky I was to have met a guy like Martin. He was my Viking. Literally. Of pure Norwegian stock. There wasn't anything he couldn't do. There still isn't.

That's not to say that we haven't had our ups and downs, but I really can't imagine my life without Martin.

So did he buy me an extravagant piece of jewelry? No. Did he surprise me with a spot for my bicycle in the garage? No. Did he get me an anniversary present? You bet he did.

He picked up a pizza and a Caesar salad (because he knows I like it), and watched a movie with me on Netflix.

It was perfect.

Goodnight, Dear Diary

37. THE ORACLE

Friday, June 10

Dear Diary:

Well, I've had a weird day.

Sophie's son, Tony, doesn't have a job. Actually, Tony has never had a job. Not even a part-time job in high school. He is twenty-three years old, the same age as Joey. Although they went to school together most of their lives, Tony and Joey were never really friends. Truthfully, Joey was never one of the "cool" boys and Tony was a major athlete. He now lives in Sophie and Dave's basement. He has a University degree in Classics (a surprise to everyone) and he is a great guy. He is funny, he is smart and he is well socialized. Tony is the first one to help any of the neighbors, which comes in handy because he is about six-foot two and one hundred and eighty pounds.

However, I can't help but think that allowing him to slide into the life of landed gentry isn't really doing Tony any favors. Sophie and Dave obviously went to a different school of parenting than Martin and I did. As nice as he is, I would have long since insisted that Tony start taking some responsibility for himself. But Sophie isn't me, and "common sense" is an oxymoron. Even at my age I continue to be surprised when I discover that people actually believe the exact opposite of what I had always assumed was generally accepted wisdom.

Anyway, I think Sophie just likes having Tony around, and doesn't seem to see that the longer she encourages him to cling, the more likely it is that her future will include a forty-year-old baby.

More to the point, not only is Sophie likely to have a forty-year-old baby in her future, as it turns out, she actually does have a real baby in her future; a grandchild. That's right; Tony's twenty-year-old girlfriend, Jessica, is pregnant. Sophie told me this afternoon.

And she didn't whisper under her breath, "Oh my God, Tony just told me Jessica is pregnant." She squealed, "I'm so excited! We just found out Tony's going to be a Daaad!" To which I could think of no response other than, "Hmm." I know, not wildly gracious of me, but I honestly had no idea what to say.

As it turned out, I didn't really need to say much of anything, because Sophie couldn't stop gushing about her "exciting" news. They're going to renovate the walkout basement and Jessica is going to move in. They'll add a bedroom for the baby, a big new bathroom, a living area and a kitchenette. "It'll be like their own apartment with a separate entrance."

I finally thought of something to say, "I guess you've really thought this through." Which didn't even remotely reflect what I really wanted to say, which was, "Snap out of it! This is a disaster! What are you thinking?"

Certain things in life are just true. And one of them is that people don't really want advice from anyone. If they can't even be counted on to follow the advice they pay for (ask any lawyer or accountant), how much influence do you think you're really going to have if you're handing it out for free? So I try not to give any. It saves everyone a lot of grief.

"Of course you and Martin are invited."

"Invited?"

"Tony wants to have all the neighbors over, you know, to introduce them to Jessica. Make her feel at home. So we thought we'd do a big 4th of July party at our house."

Wow. If it were me, the last thing I would want is for my unemployed son's pregnant girlfriend to "feel at home" in my basement (possibly even in my neighborhood).

"So can you guys come?"

"Let me just check with Martin, but yeah, we'd love to come." (Not altogether happy about adding to my showering schedule, but...)

"Oh, and no gifts."

"No gifts?" (Not even some free advice?)

"No, absolutely no gifts. Tony insists. Oh, and guess what they've decided to name the baby."

"... I can't imagine."

"It's a name that can be used for either a boy or a girl."

"Really? ...Sandy? Chris? Pat?"

"No. You'll never guess... It's Delphi."

"Delphi... Hmm... Really... A boy or a girl... Interesting." (Read "WTF".)

And after Sophie skipped happily back to the nest she was reinforcing, I couldn't help but wonder what a quick consult with the as yet unborn Delphi might reveal: *"If the threshold is crossed over forever in turmoil will five lives be."*

That's the problem with oracles; you have to be very careful how you interpret them.

Goodnight, Dear Diary. (And no, it's not the same as Grace getting divorced and moving back in with me.)

38. DO YOU SEE WHAT I SEE?

Sunday, June 12

Dear Diary:

If there is one thing that retirement affords me, it is the opportunity to contemplate. And what I spent today contemplating was schizophrenia.

What led me to start thinking about schizophrenia was actually Martin's REM Sleep Disorder. With Martin's sleep disorder, his brain has a malfunctioning "I'm asleep now" switch that is supposed to essentially paralyze a person's voice and body when they are asleep (for obvious reasons). Because his switch doesn't work properly, when he is asleep he can speak in a normal voice and carry on conversations (his end of them at least). He can also act out (in a limited way) some of his dreams. In other words, he is able to be factually asleep and dreaming while one control center in his brain behaves as if he is still awake.

So I started thinking about schizophrenics who see and hear things that aren't real. Is it possible that they have the opposite problem of Martin? That is, maybe their brains have a malfunctioning "I'm awake now" switch that is supposed to stop the brain from creating dreams when they are fully conscious. In other words, maybe they are not having hallucinations and hearing voices when they are awake, maybe they are experiencing actual dreams while they are fully conscious.

Think of all the bizarre things, people and other creatures we fabricate say and do in our dreams; the unrealistic scenarios that occur in a dream state that could never happen in real life. If, as you were going about your daily life, your brain started playing all your dreams for you, and you had no explanation for what was going on, wouldn't you start exhibiting very strange behavior and mood problems? Wouldn't you start to feel paranoid and aggressive? Wouldn't you start to feel crazy? Wouldn't people observing you think you were acting crazy?

With apologies to the experts who know that it flies in the face of conventional wisdom and is likely, ridiculous, my theory is that what we call schizophrenia may actually be just another sleep disorder.

I wonder what would happen if a schizophrenic was taken off all their medications, and it was explained to them that they are not crazy, that they simply happen to have a sleep disorder that allows them to dream while they are conscious.

Could they not be helped to find a way to sort out the difference between things that are happening in their "awake dreams" from things that are happening in their real life? There is far less stigma associated with having a rare sleep disorder than with being labeled crazy, which is a good beginning in and of itself. Add to that the fact that schizophrenics could be given a perfectly rational explanation for what is happening to them, and you never know what might be possible.

I do know that people with REM Sleep Disorder can have poorer quality sleep than the average person. Maybe improving the quality of sleep a schizophrenic experiences would help control the "I'm awake now" switch.

I would be interested in knowing whether the part of the brain that is active during a dream state is also active during a schizophrenic's "hallucinations".

Just a fully conscious thought.

Sweet dreams, Dear Diary.

39. SUZY HOMEMAKER

Wednesday, June 15

Dear Diary:

I've been trying to get this whole "housekeeping" thing under control, and it's very difficult.

I can tell you one thing, it gives me new respect for my Mother. Our house was always clean when I was a kid. The bathrooms were clean, the carpets were vacuumed, the furniture was polished, the floors were washed (and waxed - remember those days), the laundry was done, the cooking and cleaning were done, and every once in a while Mom would defrost the freezer and clean out the fridge. And she never seemed to make much of a fuss about any of it. In fact, until recently, I had no idea how much effort and organization it must have actually taken.

Fortunately, when I was working all day, Martin wasn't any fussier than I was. Of course we always had food to eat and the laundry was washed (although many mornings were spent hunting through the "clean" baskets for underwear and socks). And of course we'd wipe down the bathrooms whenever one of us found them too gross to use, but that was basically it. If guests were coming, Martin would vacuum and I would run a cloth over the furniture. But on the whole, our house was probably somewhere between messy and livable most of the time. On a scale of one to ten, we operated regularly at about a three and ramped it up to maybe a six or seven if company was coming.

You'll recall that I did make up that schedule for everything, including housework, a while back. Well, that didn't last. Correction, it never actually got implemented. But I've come to the conclusion that now that I am retired, we (read "I") have to try to set a new standard for housekeeping.

I like to call that new standard "fairly sensible". I am never going to be Suzy Homemaker. That simply isn't going to happen. I just can't take housework seriously enough to devote the time and energy required to keep up with anybody else in that department, let alone be the gifted student of homemaking. But maybe, just maybe, I can get it up to a constant five. If I could keep everything running at a five I think that would be good. I'm going for a "C minus". It's not that I couldn't get an "A" if I put my mind to it, I just don't want to put my mind to it. Much like achievement in any field, be it scholastics, art, music or athletics, the ability and the opportunity alone do not result in success, one must also have the inclination. It is the inclination that I lack.

So, with that goal in mind, I have resolved to clean the bathrooms, vacuum the carpets and polish the furniture once a week from here on in. Not all at once, of course. It's much more tolerable if I spread it out over a few days.

Well, must off to bed - tomorrow is windowsill day.

Goodnight, Dear Diary.

40. FINE YOUNG CANNIBALS

Monday, June 20

Dear Diary:

Martin was talking to someone on the phone today, and I overheard him say, "She drives me crazy." I'm going to go out on a limb here, and assume that he was talking about me. Well, it had to be me, Lucy, or given in response to the question, "What was that great song by the Fine Young Cannibals?"

For some reason, I couldn't get his comment out of my mind. Don't get me wrong; the issue was not that he might tell someone that I drive him crazy. I actually get that. What I couldn't get out of my mind was the question, "Is it possible to literally drive someone crazy?"

Again, back when I was working, that statement would have gone in one ear and out the other, but now that I am retired, remarks like that can take on a whole life of their own. Maybe it's because my brain has so little else to really focus on, but I find questions like that come into my head all the time.

I know we all use "drives me crazy" as an expression. We don't mean it to be taken literally. But what I find myself pondering is the question, "Can you actually drive another person crazy?" If so, is there a limit to the kind of crazy you can drive them? Like, can you drive someone specifically bipolar? How would you do that? Would you do something different to drive someone narcissistic? Obsessive-compulsive? Psychotic? Can you make someone have a multiple personality disorder?

If you look at the whole nurture vs. nature argument, there is probably some evidence to suggest that you can literally drive someone crazy. Which means that each of us has at our disposal a rather formidable power. Of course it would have to be done over a significant period of time. I doubt you could make somebody crazy over the short term. You would need years of sustained influence over the person; preferably a person who hadn't already developed a personality.

Hmm. I probably should have thought about this before raising two kids.

Think I'll call Grace and see how she's doing.
Goodnight, Dear Diary.

41. TMI

Thursday, June 23

Dear Diary:

Took a look in my 20X magnification mirror this morning. Not a good way to start the day. Too much information. Normally I imagine myself looking relatively sensible for my age, but after looking into that stupid mirror, my brain couldn't stop fixating on all my facial flaws. I couldn't get them out of my head even when I wasn't anywhere near a mirror. I felt like one of those "apple-head" dolls that creep out little children.

It was so depressing that I had to think up something to do to make myself feel better and get that image out of my head, so I spent a good part of the afternoon dancing around the living room lip-synching to some awesome dance songs.

Take note: if you are planning a party where you want people to dance, there is some music that I defy anyone to sit still for. I'm not saying that these are the best songs of all time, or even that they are my favorite songs. They are just songs that nobody can hear without at the very least tapping their toes (if not playing air instruments while remaining seated on the couch). In order of release date, they are:

1. *Heat Wave* (Martha and the Vandellas, 1963),
2. *Chain of Fools* (Aretha Franklin, 1967),
3. *Street Fighting Man* (The Rolling Stones, 1968),
4. *Dance To The Music* (Sly & The Family Stone, 1968) *
5. *I Want You Back* (The Jackson 5, 1969),
6. *Signed, Sealed, Delivered, I'm Yours* (Stevie Wonder, 1970),
7. *Locomotive Breath* (Jethro Tull, 1971),
8. *Billie Jean* (Michael Jackson, 1982),
9. *Sharp Dressed Man* (ZZ Top, 1983),
10. *Sabotage* (Beastie Boys, 1994),
11. *Family Affair* (Mary J. Blige, 2001)
12. *Everybody Got Their Something* (Nikka Costa, 2001),
13. *Africa* (Karl Wolf version, 2007),
14. *Numb/Encore* (Linkin Park, Jay-Z, 2008),
15. *New Divide* (Linkin Park, 2009).

Felt so good afterwards that I actually made dinner - tuna melts.

* Note: for decades I was convinced that one of the lines in *Dance To The Music* was "I'm gonna add some baritone, so they could dance with just one eye."

As it turns out, the line is really "I'm gonna add some bottom so that the dancers just won't hide."

Quite frankly, I think my version is way more funky. I can actually envision people dancing "with just one eye". It not only makes complete sense to me, it was possibly my favorite line in the entire song. One of my favorite lyrics ever. I'm also pretty sure I've seen people dancing "with just one eye".

Should they change the lyrics? You tell me.

Goodnight, Dear Diary. #dancewithjustoneeye

42. PICK A SPOT; ANY SPOT

Tuesday, June 28

Dear Diary:

Possibly the best thing ever about being retired? Shopping in the middle of the week! I don't mean rushing to the pharmacy or window-shopping at the mall on your lunch hour, I mean full on, take-your-time, try-on-merchandise shopping that you can start at 10:45 a.m. and go until you "feel" like leaving.

And the very best part of all of that? You can pull into the Costco parking lot and not have to drive around for ten minutes trying to find a spot. Or worse, park in the spot reserved for pregnant women and stick your belly out as far as you can. Okay, I've never really done that, but I have given it serious consideration on occasion. God, how I hated going to Costco on Saturdays and Sundays.

And when you shop on the weekend, you never seem to be able to try out any of the samples being given out. I love samples. I always hated waiting in line for what looked and smelled like a very tasty morsel of food only to have the toaster oven lady say when it was my turn, "Sorry, come back in about five minutes." But on a weekday, the toaster oven lady is actually calling you over to try out one of her samples. "Go ahead, dear. Take two." I love samples. I have yet to taste a sample that I didn't like – and buy. Obviously Costco has figured out that if they give away samples, people will buy whatever it is they're flogging. It works for me. Without Costco samples I would never even have known about Popcorners, Collier's Welsh cheddar cheese or Kozy Shack rice pudding.

But just as importantly, when you shop during the week you get to take as much time as you want strolling through the spacious aisles looking at everything. Instead of fighting your way around families of twelve and dawdlers in a crowded aisle on a Saturday, you get to do the dawdling yourself. Of course that puts you at greater risk of being "ten dollared" to death, "Honey. Look at this. It's only $9.95." But so worth it.

Do you know that I can't even remember what shopping was like before Costco (B.C.)? We must have gone somewhere. But it was probably a lot less fun.

Well, goodnight, Dear Diary. I have sixty rolls of toilet paper to put in the basement.

P.S. Possible downside to being retired? On the way into the store from the parking lot, Martin leaned into me and whispered, "Isn't that the T-shirt you wore to bed last night?" Oops.

43. VELCRO SANDALS

Thursday, June 30

Dear Diary:

Only a few short months ago I considered myself to be a pretty classy dresser. No, I didn't own any Manolo Blahnik or Jimmy Choo shoes, but I always bought "good" business attire on sale.

Now, not only does most of my wardrobe not fit me, even if it did, nobody buys groceries in a wool gabardine suit unless they are on their way home from work. I know I used to dress up for Walmart, but since Charles started working there I don't even bother doing that anymore. I have nowhere to wear ninety percent of my clothing. I've bought (and not returned) two new pairs of jeans, one pair of khakis and one pair of black stretch Capri pants. At least all the weight I gained didn't affect my T-shirt or sweater size. I know, not a pretty picture.

Almost overnight, I've gone from leaving the house in a black wool gabardine suit, a crisp white blouse and black leather pumps, to heading out the door in jeans, hoodies and sandals that are held together by Velcro. I feel like I don't even know who I am anymore. I've stopped wearing make-up, flat ironing my hair and generally bothering with what I look like. What's next? Baggy sweat pants and flip-flops? A purple velour tracksuit and white sneakers?

It's been so depressing looking at all my work clothes, that today I just decided to get rid of them. Shoes included. When am I ever going to need to wear sling-back pumps again? I held onto one black suit and my best pair of black shoes (yes, in case anybody dies), folded the rest and put them in plastic bins in the basement. I'm not quite ready to actually give them away. Who knows - I might get that paper route.

So now when I look in the closet there is one black suit, one cream colored jersey top, two dresses for special occasions, one pair of dressy shoes, one pair of black pumps, a pair of track shoes, a pair of Velcro sandals and my old sheepskin slippers.

Let's face it, unless it's New Year's Eve or I'm going to a funeral, I don't need to ever open my closet again except to grab a pair of shoes. And for the first time in my life I could actually live without a closet. How is that possible? I've spent my entire life fighting for closet space and all of a sudden I could get away with a small shoe rack on a shelf somewhere. This just doesn't feel right.

I had no idea how much of an impact retiring would have on my sense of who I am. I always thought that was a "guy thing". I thought women derived their sense of identity from everything but their jobs. But I was wrong. I was very much what I did. And now I don't know who I am anymore.

Maybe I shouldn't have retired. Maybe all I needed was a long vacation.

This must be the exact opposite of how someone who goes through a sex change feels. In their cases, they spend their whole lives not identifying with the person they see in the mirror, the clothes they wear and the way they have to behave with family, friends and colleagues. Then all of a sudden they finally get to feel and act like "themselves". No wonder they don't care what anybody else thinks. They can finally "be" who they are.

But I don't even know who I am anymore. It feels like I am now nobody. I can't be a housewife. That isn't me. It never was. I'm no longer a Mom in the real sense of the word; the kids are gone. Yes, I'm Martin's wife, whatever that means. I'm starting to understand why people who retire sometimes don't thrive.

How do the rich do it? Really, how do they define themselves? Is just being rich enough? I mean, they can go anywhere, buy anything, and undertake any activity they want, but is that enough? Does that give them a sense of identity? A sense of self? "Bill's a teacher, Judy's a botanist and Jeff...oh, Jeff's rich." That doesn't work. Even the Royals have duties. Maybe that's how philanthropy started – not out of a sense of compassion for people in need as much as out of a need to have something to do.

It's funny how there is no relationship between a sense of self-worth and how much you are worth financially.

Well, Dear Diary, this is actually making me feel even more depressed than looking in my closet. I have to go and lie down.

Goodnight.

44. INDEPENDENCE DAY

Monday, July 4

Dear Diary:

Just got back from Sophie and Dave's party for Tony and Jessica, who is really very pretty and seems genuinely nice. She sort of put me in mind of a young Meg Ryan; not what I had pictured at all. Although at times she might have been a little overwhelmed by the crowd, Tony was all smiles, proudly showing her off to all and sundry and making a point of letting us all know that they are "expecting". All we can do at this stage, I guess, is just hope that everything works out for them. Maybe it will. Not sure if Jessica noticed, but Sophie was acting like she is the one "expecting".

Charles and Daphne were there, still acting every bit the Lord and Lady of the manor, and nobody even mentioned Charles' new "position" with Walmart. It may have had something to do with the minor fracas that erupted when Charles claimed to have been cornered in the powder room by a wasp (pretty sure he wasn't trying to be satirical). My guess? It gave Charles something other than Walmart to talk about whenever it appeared he was going to be engaged in conversation.

Anyway, Sophie wanted to go over all the plans for the renovation of the basement walkout with me in great detail. And, apart from the fact that the irony of gushing over the renovation of her basement for her twenty-three-year-old son and his pregnant girlfriend on Independence Day appeared to be lost on her, I was also a bit taken aback by some of her comments. All the countertops in the bathroom and kitchenette are going to be granite "of course", and all the appliances just have to be "high-end".

I'm beginning to wonder if I've lost touch with reality or if everybody else has. I get so tired of seeing home renovation shows where every kid who works at a fast-food place feels they have to start life with "high-end" appliances, hardwood floors, granite countertops and everything "open concept".

We are sixty years old, have lived in this house for over twenty years, and still don't have any of those things. In the first place, I don't even like "open concept". Don't people understand that after kids turn five, maybe you don't always want to see them from every corner of the house? I like rooms. I don't want everybody watching me chop spinach or peel potatoes. The kitchen is my workspace. It is where the mess is. I don't want it to be on display to everyone who steps in the front door.

And although we did replace one stained and chipped melamine bathroom countertop (as you know) with another melamine bathroom countertop, we've never upgraded our kitchen or bathrooms. They work fine the way they are. We have linoleum tiles in the kitchen and bathrooms, and carpet everywhere else. Dogs can't run on hardwood floors.

Maybe I'm weird, but there are certain very specific things that I think make a house a home, and granite countertops, high-end appliances and hardwood floors don't make my list. To be more specific, if I could have everything I ever wanted in a house, my list would be this:

1. Wood burning fireplace: I don't want to flip a switch on a wall and have an instant "fire". If flames alone make you feel all cozy, you might as well just turn on your high-end gas stove or light a candle. I like the smell and the crackle of real wood and pinecones burning.

2. Clothesline: And I don't mean one of those bogus umbrella-style clothes hangers, I mean an actual clothesline that extends between two posts.

3. Covered Verandah: Sitting or lounging in the shade of a covered verandah on a warm summer day. Add a cold drink and a good book, and life doesn't get much better than that.

4. Untreated Cedar Deck: I don't want the deck to be an unending make-work project, which is what it will be the minute you decide to stain it, treat it or paint it. Let the cedar grey naturally. It will be lovely and maintenance-free. Pressure-treated lumber is not safe for the animals. Period.

5. Basketball Hoop: The hoop rim must be regulation height, ten feet above the ground. It must be on a regulation backboard mounted over the garage door. It cannot be one of those so-called portable basketball hoops that end up looking like discarded junk at the end of your driveway and invariably present a road hazard to all of your neighbors.

6. Fenced Yard: Again, think maintenance-free. Unless you can

afford wrought iron, black chain link blends best into the background and doesn't make you feel claustrophobic the way a solid fence can. It also allows the dog to see what's on the other side of the fence and bark as required. It must be six feet high.

7. Central Vacuum: Dogs, cats, carpets. Need I say more?

8. Screen Door: Look for the spring-hinged variety that makes that great "clacking" sound when it shuts. This is not a security measure. Govern yourself accordingly.

9. Unfinished Basement: Ideally, a basement should not be a living space. It is underground. It is where you do your laundry and store the Christmas decorations, lawn furniture, camping equipment and all the stuff that you want to throw out but are saving for the garage sale that will never take place. It is the place where your kids will find all the boxes of old photographs and family memorabilia when you are being shuffled into a nursing home. And if you don't have an unfinished basement, where else is Martin, I mean your husband, going to put most of his junk?

10. Touchtone Kitchen Wall Phone: Preferably in avocado. The nostalgia factor far outweighs the inconvenience.

11. Two Refrigerators: If you like cold drinks or shop at Costco you will need a second refrigerator.

12. Flagpole.

When we were young, Martin and I had a hand-me-down chesterfield that looked like a bench seat from a car, some used milk crates to house our albums, shelves made of bricks and boards and a few cushions on the floor.

Today, everybody seems to "need" everything they see in Architectural Digest. We liked to look at all the cool stuff too, but never really aspired to having what we assumed was reserved for millionaires.

I mean seriously, how does a kitchen go out of style? Unless something breaks, why does a bathroom need "updating"? It's a bathroom. If you aren't charging people admittance, then it's actually not a spa. Does it have a bathtub and a sink and a toilet? Are they working? Then you should be all set. And I actually have a soft spot for kitchens from the 1940s and bathrooms from the 1960s (remember turquoise toilets and sinks).

Of course a house needs to be maintained. You will need new windows, new shingles and a new furnace. The carpeting will also wear out and need to be replaced. Those things are expensive, and that is why spending tens of thousands of dollars on change for the sake of change is not my thing and, quite frankly, I don't understand it. Most people do not have money to throw away. We sure don't, and we've had two pretty good careers for a very long time.

I may be ranting. Sorry. Better go to bed now (and no, we didn't upgrade to a King-sized bed).

Goodnight, Dear Diary.

45. FARTING BARBIE

Wednesday, July 6

Dear Diary:

I'm not sure if it's because I've had babies on the brain since the party, but I've come up with a few new doll ideas I'm thinking of sending off to Mattel.

Although I leave it to Mattel to come up with the most marketable names, my first idea is to create a "Farting Barbie". Basically, every time you raise her arms up, she farts. Isn't it about time little girls had a more realistic role model?

Farting Barbie aside, I suspect the biggest seller would be what I like to call "Chatty Husband". Using a remote control, you can make him say, "You look gorgeous." "Have you lost weight?" "Let me take care of that." "You are absolutely right." or "I apologize." I realize this may give little girls the entirely wrong impression about what male/female relationships look like in real life, but let's face it, did any of us actually marry a Ken?

In a similar vein, I'm pretty sure "Reliable Boyfriend" would be a winner. He is identical to "Chatty Husband" with one exception, you can program him to call at least once a day. I think little girls deserve to know where the bar should be set.

Last, but far from being least, would be a doll for adults. Get your mind out of the gutter. I'm talking about "Happy Teenager", which would be available in both "boy" and "girl" models and sit studiously in a corner and smile all day. These dolls don't speak. Ever. With a Happy Teenager doll, any parent who wants to put the latest teen crisis out of their minds can simply talk about their Happy Teenager when they are out with their friends whose kids are all beautiful, well-balanced, mature, problem-free and excel at everything. "Yes, your son does sound wonderful. Our "Josh" is also extremely studious - never complains about anything. That kid is smiling from morning 'til night. Such a pleasure."

And I thought my working days were over.

Goodnight, Dear Diary.

46. GOLDFISH

Sunday, July 10

Dear Diary:

The Internet knows who I am. And it's a little unsettling.

Yes, I want to know the five warning signs of a stroke, I just don't want the Internet to know that I want to know the five warning signs of a stroke. But these windows keep popping up every time I am on the Internet, and they are all things I actually find interesting (although I did go down one rabbit hole today where I found myself looking at twenty movie stars who didn't age well, celebrities who have hideous spouses, plastic surgery mishaps and actors who have become obese).

I can be innocently searching for bamboo placemats one minute, and then find myself three hours later watching YouTube clips of wedding mishaps. It's no wonder our attention spans have dropped to eight seconds. Even goldfish have an attention span of nine seconds.

So the next time somebody asks you why you don't appear to be "accomplishing" anything – blame the Internet. I do. Damn you, Al Gore.

Goodnight, Dear Diary.

47. LET THERE BE LIGHT

Thursday, July 14

Dear Diary:

Sitting here looking out our bedroom window tonight, I have to give Martin credit. He is one of those guys who, when he sets his mind to it, can actually do anything.

The brick pedestal lights at the end of our driveway have been pretty wonky for quite some time, with one tilting right about fifteen degrees and the other tilting backwards at about a ten degree angle. Although I never really paid much attention, it drove Martin crazy. In truth, they did tend to give our house something of a "Munster's" air.

But those days are gone. Thanks to Martin, we now have tall, black lampposts with triple lantern lights flanking our driveway. And the other ten exterior lights on the house have all been changed to match. Equipped with a staggering 16 brilliant outdoor LED light bulbs (which Martin has set to turn on and off at dusk and dawn), our house is now possibly visible from space at night.

The neighbors literally stop and stare as they walk or drive past, the deer avoid our house like it's a Walmart parking lot, and I'm convinced that if I stood at the end of our one hundred-foot driveway with a pair of marshalling wands, I could actually guide aircraft to a safe landing.

Who needs to see the stars anyway?

Goodnight Dear Diary.

48. 98.9°

Monday, July 18

Dear Diary

Color me disappointed. Not because I had that all-over-achy feeling that usually signals a cold has arrived, but because I had that all-over-achy feeling that usually signals a cold has arrived - and I derived absolutely no benefit from it.

At least when I was working I had options. I could suffer through and go to work and get sympathy. Or, having satisfied myself that I really was sick (or having a hot flash) with a temperature of 98.9°, I could call in sick and snuggle under the duvet all day with pots of hot tea and a good book. It always made me deliriously happy to know that I didn't have to get up and fight traffic - sort of like a long weekend but better, because I didn't feel like I had to "do something" to memorialize the extra time off. No outings to arrange, no guests for dinner, no super sales to attend. Aaahh. As long as you weren't "too" sick, taking a sick day was always great.

But for retired people - let me say this - first of all, it took me a few hours to even realize that I had that all-over-achy feeling that usually signals a cold has arrived. It could just as easily have been that I had stayed up too late watching T.V. or was simply feeling less than inspired to get out of bed. So by the time I knew for sure that I was actually sick (fever, chills, slightly sore throat) I had already completed a number of my daily retirement tasks (feeding the cat, fixing Mr. Boogie's cage, emptying the dishwasher). There was no day off.

At least when I was working, feeling like crap had a bit of an "up" side. When you are retired and feel like crap all you have is the feeling like crap part - possibly followed by a doctor's appointment, which only further interferes with your retirement (and throws off your showering schedule).

In fact, not only does a sick day not give a retiree any benefits, we have so much time on our hands that it can leave you feeling not only sick, but also pissed-off and slightly vulnerable. Is it just a cold? What are the symptoms of heart failure, anyway? Throat cancer? Emphysema? Let's face it; a sick, retired person with access to the

Internet is nothing short of a prescription for Lorazepam waiting to happen.

I tried going back to bed and pretending I was staying home sick from work, but I was too frustrated. Retirement takes all the fun out of being sick.

Goodnight, Dear Diary.

49. MAO REVISITED

Wednesday, July 20

Dear Diary:

According to my Mother, I was a little bit "different" as a child.

Apparently, I thought washing, detangling, brushing, braiding, trimming and generally tending to my waist-length hair was a stupid waste of time and effort. My solution? I announced to the family that it would make much more sense if we all just shaved our heads. I was eight.

And I didn't stop there. I was also convinced (and therefore tried to convince the entire family) that the whole clothing issue should be dramatically simplified. "All our clothes should be the same color." And, "Why don't they make clothes that don't need zippers or buttons?"

So, was my behavior born of an innate asceticism that belied my years? Truthfully, I suspect that it was more because I was either a slow learner or just plain lazy when it came to hair management, color coordination and lining buttons up with the right button holes. I also seem to remember my mother complaining that I was forever "breaking" zippers, although I don't specifically recall exactly how I was managing to do that. But a kid can only be "reminded" so many times that brown socks don't "go" with a navy blue skirt before they just want to throw in the towel out of frustration.

Not surprisingly, nobody listened to me. And as I grew up, I gradually came to appreciate why. I recall that when I was eleven, there was going to be no consoling me if I didn't get that bubble-gum pink mohair sweater from the catalogue for my birthday. And at fourteen, all my girlfriends were jealous when I was the first girl to have baby-blue corduroy "hot pants" with a button fly. Predictably, style choices got even more complicated as I went through my teens and twenties, which featured more than my share of fashion faux pas (I may be the only person alive who ever actually bought a stretch terry jumpsuit). But, eventually I outgrew my "fad phase" and developed what I like to believe was a real sense of style.

While somewhat on the conservative side, probably largely due to my profession, I made a point of keeping up with age-appropriate fashion trends and hair styles and took pride in maintaining a current look. Truth to tell, I even sometimes looked down my nose on middle-aged women who seemed oblivious to the fact that permed hair, acid-wash jeans and giant shoulder pads hadn't been in style for decades. "Oh this? I've had this for thirty years." Like we would never have guessed. And I couldn't understand why any woman ever believed that short hair made her look younger the day after she turned forty. It doesn't make you look younger. It makes you look like a forty-year-old with short hair. Short hair is only flattering on the very young, and even then you have to be pretty good looking to pull it off.

So what is my point? As difficult as it is to accept, I seem to have come full circle. And I am starting to believe that the mere act of retiring has had a real effect on the sense of style I spent a lifetime developing and once took such pride in. I don't mean that I've just switched from a working wardrobe to a casual wardrobe. What I mean is…well, judge for yourself:

1. If you were to meet me on the street and ask me to close my eyes, I probably couldn't tell you what I was wearing.
2. If you were to meet me on the street three days later I would probably still be wearing the same thing.
3. Everything I own could be classed as "transition wear". Which is to say that I wear the same things to bed that I wear to Walmart and the grocery store.
4. None of my pants have zippers.
5. I haven't been to the dry cleaner in five months.
6. I have no idea when or where I last saw my iron.
7. I canceled my last three hairdresser appointments.
8. My feet are a half size bigger than they were.
9. Three tank tops, four T-shirts and two of Martin's old hoodies have replaced my shirts, blouses and sweaters.
10. "Good hair" days are a thing of the past. There are only "ponytail" days and "ball cap" days. And I am considering shaving my head.

There. I've said it. I'm not proud of it. I am going to bed now. Fortunately, I don't have to change.

Goodnight, Dear Diary.

50. TAKE TWO ASPIRIN

Friday, July 22

Dear Diary:

Okay. Under the category "Things I Was Almost Positive Could Never Kill Me", migraine headaches would have been right up there with snorkeling.

I have migraines. Worse, I have migraines with aura. Annoying? Definitely. Debilitating? Sometimes. But deadly? Say what?

Clearly it pays to read the Obituaries every day, because up until this morning I had absolutely no idea that a person could actually die from "complications related to migraines". As with the snorkeling stories, the bereaved were understandably reluctant to disclose the actual details, but the same affliction I have had all my life has killed a young man in his twenties.

I racked my brain trying to imagine what those "complications" might have been. Got dizzy and fell in front of a bus? Lay down to rest on a sofa bed that snapped closed on him? Wore sunglasses indoors, tripped and banged his head on a marble coffee table? What the hell could it have been?

Yes, there have been times when I have cursed the Internet, but if you need medical information urgently your choices are limited. Do you make a doctor's appointment? Trundle down to your local library to conduct research? Hell, no. At least one of those activities requires non-essential showering. So I did what everybody does - I Googled it.

And I am shocked by my findings. Apparently it is a myth that migraines (especially with aura) are benign, non life-threatening disorders. More people died last year from migraine-related strokes than were murdered by handguns. That's right. All this time I have been locking our doors at night and making sure to park in well-lit lots, oblivious to the fact that I am a personal walking time bomb. "Step away from the old lady! She could go off any second now!"

It would appear that migraines can and do induce a whole host of "serious physical conditions":

1. Strokes,
2. Aneurysms,

3. Permanent loss of vision,

5. Severe dental problems (I know - raises more questions than it answers),

6. Coma, and

7. Death (not sure that death is so much a "serious physical condition" as a serious "lack" of physical condition - maybe just semantics).

Anyway, according to the *New England Journal of Medicine*, almost thirty percent of all strokes suffered by persons under the age of forty-five are caused by Migraines, and stroke is the third leading cause of death in this country. In addition, the Mayo clinic says that twenty-five percent of all incidents of cerebral infarction were associated with Migraines.

This is important information. Why hasn't one of my doctors ever told me about this? What do I do with this information? Should I speak to somebody about it? Tell Martin to keep a closer eye on me?

I'm feeling particularly fragile tonight. Think I'll take two aspirin and go to bed. I am definitely going to take myself more seriously from now on.

Goodnight, Dear Diary.

51. NINJA GRANNY

Sunday, July 24

Dear Diary:

Martin has been referring to me all night as "ninja granny". And although the word "granny" does speak to my age (if not my legal status), it is the "ninja" part that probably begs explanation. Maybe you'll understand once I tell you what happened today.

You see, Martin has a 1968 Chris Craft Commander 35 with twin 427 V8 engines. Yes, it may qualify as a yacht, and we are members of a yacht club, but don't get too excited. As with many things Martin holds onto, it is a work-in-progress. In fact, I believe he holds dearest those things that give him an opportunity to apply his engineering skills. While he was educated as an engineer, and has worked primarily in the area of software development for decades, at heart, he is a tinker. I say that, not to deride his abilities, but to give you a realistic sense of who he is. There isn't anything Martin cannot do, from plumbing and wiring, to creating replacement parts for his boat out of UHMW polyethylene on his milling machine. Essentially, he is a twelve-year-old boy with a lot of education, a great deal of skill and every tool you could imagine. I know he's still twelve because I'm the one who empties out his jeans pockets every time I do the laundry. I find everything but pollywogs in there. And he is never happier than when something mechanical breaks down. Before we do anything as cavalier as running out to buy a new clothes dryer to replace our twenty-year-old model that has stopped working, Martin will take the motor apart and fix it. Yes, fix it. Plenty of people enjoy taking motors apart; few can actually put them back together in working order.

On nice days when he decides he can take a day off and wants to test out his latest repairs or innovations, Martin and I head out on the river for a few hours. We leave the house mid-morning, bring lunch, and basically just enjoy the sun, the water and the wind in our hair. Today, we invited Sophie and Dave to join us. I made chicken wings and coleslaw and threw in a bag of baby carrots and some grapes. Sophie brought egg salad sandwiches, potato chips and banana bread.

I have to say, every time we drive into the yacht club towards our boat, I feel tremendously at peace. There is something about water and boats that make you feel like you are alive. I imagine a farmer feels much the same way as he surveys his acreage from the driver's seat of a combine, or a rancher when he saddles up.

One of my favorite moments is when we are all settled on our deck chairs and Martin turns on the engines, one at a time. I know sailing may be more environmentally considerate, but there is something about the sound of those big engines that continues to thrill. Martin's boat is like the Harley Davidson of the river, and with more than a hundred gallons of gas in the tanks, we can do a lot more than just putter.

Martin (or "Admiral", as I am inclined to call him on board) is in charge of virtually everything in, on, and around the boat. I have absolutely no responsibilities on board. None, that is, until the excursion has come to an end and Martin is in the process of painstakingly docking the boat in our sixteen-foot-wide slip.

As he slowly approaches the slip, with our dock on the port side, my job is to edge my way up the port side of the boat and drop the fenders off the deck, grab and hold onto the bow line, edge my way back towards the stern, stop half way, make sure the bow line is slack, place my feet one in front of the other on the rim of the deck outside the cables that run the length of the boat, jump about five feet down onto the floating dock while still holding on to the line, pull the line taught so Martin doesn't crash into the stone wall at the end of the slip, throw Martin the stern line from the dock - and voila!
I know. It sounds pretty straightforward.

Except that today, I had a bit of a premonition on approach that something could go awry. At about a hundred yards from the slip, I tried to imagine what I would do if I hit the dock wrong. In my mind, the answer was simple enough - I've seen plenty of movies where people jump over fences and leap off the sides of dumpsters, moving aircraft and small buildings. How hard could it be? I would just tuck and roll to avoid any broken bones or torn ligaments. Always good to have a plan.

So, while Martin eased the boat into the slip, Dave watched him and Sophie chatted to me as I balanced on the edge of the port side, bow line in hand, waiting for the exact right moment to jump.

Perhaps it was, as Martin later suggested, a "self-fulfilling prophecy", but for sure it was the only "Hold my beer and watch this" moment in my life. The second that my feet left the deck, I knew I had jumped too soon. Error number one.

You have to understand that, while I am physically on the boat holding the bow line, the boat and I are travelling at exactly the same speed. The moment my feet leave the deck, however, the laws of physics dictate that we do not. Ergo, because I had unwittingly failed to leave enough slack in the bow line, as I jumped off the boat and it continued forward, I found myself firmly attached to the end of what had become a very taut bow line. Error number two.

Of course in a perfect world, these two separate errors might have worked to counteract each other. That is, although I had jumped too soon, the now taut line could have pulled me forward just enough to make my landing on the dock flawless. That is not what ensued.

According to Sophie, the only witness to the whole thing, my toes barely touched the end of dock. With my knees bent, she says I tucked into a ball only a split second before my entire body did a 360-degree roll off the far side of the dock and straight into the water. With what I gather closely resembled the world's first "human yo-yo" trick, I surfaced on the far side of the dock, treading water and holding on to the bow line for all I was worth, trying desperately to keep the boat from crashing into the stone wall until Martin could get to the dock and secure the stern line.

When he finally reached me, Martin was ashen. Sophie later told me that when he heard the splash the first words out of his mouth were, "This is a catastrophe!" Although he tried to convince me to swim to shallower water before trying to get out, with his help and the help of the bow line, I hoisted myself onto the dock. This, despite the fact that I was soaking wet and laughing so hard I could barely stand up straight. I thought the whole thing must have been hilarious to watch, and I couldn't get out of my head my favorite line from the *S.A.S. Survival Handbook*: If you have fallen overboard at sea, you should "swim to the nearest shipping lane". I mean, is that even a real thing? And if it is, aren't you already in one? I could go on.

Anyway, until they disembarked (via the convenience of a stepladder) and got over to us, Sophie and Dave appeared to be quite concerned. I have to say, if the roles had been reversed I'm not so sure I could have kept a straight face. But of course once everybody realized that I wasn't hurt, we all had a good laugh about it and I was dubbed "ninja granny".

On the drive home, Martin suggested that from now on I should be required to wear a helmet on board. I think he was joking. Sophie kept repeating that she couldn't believe how spry I was, which actually annoyed me - I'm pretty sure the word "spry" isn't a compliment to anyone under the age of eighty.

One thing is certain. Never in my wildest imagination did I think the services of a stunt double would be required if they ever made a movie about my life.

Well, that's the story for today, Dear Diary. It so easily could have gone another way...like with me starring in tomorrow's most perplexing Obituary.

P.S. I'm giving serious consideration to attempting a reverse four-and-a-half somersault for next week's performance.

52. COME FLY WITH ME

Wednesday, July 27

Dear Diary:

I found myself taking a little bit of pride in having emptied the dishwasher today, until I realized I was taking a little bit of pride in having emptied the dishwasher. Pretty much just self-loathing and Netflix the whole rest of the day.

But I did learn one thing. If you're ever watching a Netflix show in a foreign language with subtitles, you really can't just "close your eyes for a minute" and still understand what's going on. You think you can - but you can't.

In an unrelated thought, I spent some time watching Mr. Boogie today, and it made me really sad. I felt so sorry for him that I almost cried. I know he has it good in some ways. His cage (what a terrible word) sits inside a large bay window overlooking the woods. The windows on both sides of the bay are double-hung, so they can be opened from the top or the bottom, giving him a nice breeze when the temperature is warm enough, or letting in just the sounds of all the birds and other woodland creatures when it is cooler. He has natural branches sitting diagonally in his space so he can hop up and down the branches, which apparently is something his species likes to do. He has a bathtub, a water dish and all the food he could ever want.

But several times a day I hear him singing and chirping his little heart out, and I just know he is hoping against hope that a mate will answer him (although at twelve, I'm not sure what he would actually do with a mate). His only friend is the image of himself in the large mirror sitting just outside his house, and I've seen him "talking" to and ruffling his feathers for his friend more times than I care to count. It's almost unbearable to see him sidling up to his own reflection and trying to start up a conversation: "Hey. What's up? Care to join me for a bath? Can I get you something to eat?" But his friend never answers. And he's got no one to play with.

I also feel guilty for not having bought him another mate after his first one died, but he was already five years old, and nobody could have guessed he'd survive this long. And of course now it would just be foolhardy to bring in another young bird. It also kills me that he can't do the one thing he was born to do - fly. I wish I knew what day he was going to die. I would bring him outside and let him fly.

For me, though, the most heart-wrenching moments are when he sees people coming up the driveway to the house. He sings louder and longer then than at any other time. I'm almost positive he's trying to signal for help. "It's me, Mr. Boogie. I'm being held prisoner up here! Look up! Look up! I'm up here! Help!"

Wow. I have really, really bummed myself out. I have to go.

Goodnight, Dear Diary.

53. PLEASE FASTEN YOUR SEATBELTS

Tuesday, August 2

Dear Diary

Well, Martin's car finally died. It was a long, painful death, and we didn't feel heroic measures were any longer appropriate. When he had it towed away, Martin wouldn't even accept fifty dollars for it. It was too much of an insult to the vehicle that had once been so treasured and had given us fifteen years of service. No, better to imagine it had gone to a "farm" somewhere staffed by kindly folk who would care for it, than to think of it crushed into oblivion and left to sit amongst rusting metal carcasses in a giant industrial lot.

To Martin's credit, he didn't go out and buy himself a snazzy sports car to replace his sedan. He didn't even look at one. No, Martin had done his research, and wanted his replacement vehicle to accommodate our every conceivable need for the next fifteen years. In very short order he determined that he wanted a three-year-old vehicle that had been leased. "Why pay for all that depreciation?" He also wanted that vehicle to be a Honda. "Great engines. Great reputation." And, after literally making up pros and cons lists, he decided he wanted a Honda Pilot.

Having taken the process that far, and finding all available previously leased three-year-old Honda Pilots for sale within driving distance, Martin then turned the negotiations over to me. That's the thing about Martin. He recognizes his own strengths and weaknesses and appreciates that I do come with a specific skillset. Well, it's either that or he just doesn't like haggling.

Perhaps surprisingly, the tactics used to get a vehicle at the price you want are not wildly dissimilar to the tactics you use at a Returns counter. Never underestimate the power of an awkward silence.

But most importantly, when searching for a used vehicle you should always bear in mind that a dealership that specializes in one brand of vehicle will not want to hold on too long to a vehicle from a different manufacturer that directly competes with its own stock. Case in point: I want a Honda Pilot. Some person has taken a three-year-old leased Honda Pilot to a Ford dealership to trade it in on a new Ford Explorer. The Ford dealership now has its competitor's stock sitting on its lot. And if that vehicle has been sitting on the lot for more than thirty days, you have the makings of a great deal at a price you are willing to pay (no matter what they tell you). Done and done.

And that is precisely what happened. Martin and I are now the proud owners of a new (to us) Honda Pilot. Yes, there are only two of us. No, we don't have any grandchildren yet. But Martin has looked into the future, and sees us loading the grandkids into the two back rows of seats and sliding their favorite DVD into the entertainment system. Fifteen years, remember. A lot can happen.

Sure, Martin gets to be the Pilot, but I'm the Co-pilot. Needless to say, Lucy is the Air Marshall. I have also nominated Mr. Boogie to be the (honorary) Flight Attendant (it was the right thing to do). As for Twink - well, Twink wants nothing other than to be the passenger - as long as she is flying First Class.

Think I'll go ask Martin if he's up for a night flight. No sense wasting that beautifully lit up runway he's created.

Goodnight, Dear Diary.

54. AKIMBO

Saturday, August 6

Dear Diary:

Every once in a while I run into a word that I have never seen before, and I have to look it up. This afternoon I was reading a book and ran across the word "lacuna".

Lacuna. Lacuna. Lacuna. What a beautiful word. I couldn't recall ever seeing it before. If I had, I certainly didn't remember what it meant. But I loved it. Lacuna. I couldn't stop saying it. It made me feel like I could speak a foreign language. Lacuna.

And as I was repeating it to myself, I realized that there are a number of words that I have rather strong feelings about. There are words that I simply don't like, and there are words that I love. But my feelings about words seem to have more to do with their sounds than their meanings.

So I decided to put together a list of words that strongly affect me. I was actually startled by the length of the list. There are hundreds of words I love, and hundreds of words I hate. There were so many in both lists that I had real difficulty in narrowing them down.

But I finally came up with my five favorite words and my five least favorite words, and here they are, in descending order:

Favorite Words:

1. Akimbo: Most fun word ever. How could anybody not like the word "akimbo"? Oh, I'm sure they are out there, in the same way that once in your lifetime you'll come across someone who will actually say "I don't like bananas." But I can pretty much promise you that just saying the word "akimbo" will make you smile. And, it sounds exactly like what it means. Unfortunately, there are far too few opportunities in life for using it after your "I'm a little teapot" years are behind you.

2. Bubbles: The word "bubbles" is always entertaining. Get whoever is standing next to you to slowly say the word "bubbles" and tell me that it doesn't make you laugh out loud.

3. Resolute: Even if I didn't know what "resolute" meant I

would want to be it. Right away you know it's a serious word. There is nothing amusing or trivial about "resolute". If "resolute" had to be given a human name, it wouldn't be "Dwayne" or "Amber"; it would be something like "James" or "Helen".

4. Exponential: I always feel smart when I say "exponential". I even feel smart when I hear somebody else say "exponential". It's not the kind of word just anybody can throw around. The next time you hear somebody say "exponential", I want you to check them out. They will be wearing glasses. Guaranteed.

5. Apostolic: There is definitely something spiritual about the word "Apostolic". If you close your eyes and slowly repeat it three times, it will start to put you in a trance, like a four-syllable Christian version of the mystical Hindu mantra "Om". It is a beautiful, peaceful and calming word (unless you are unable to put the whole Spanish Inquisition thing out of your mind).

Least Favorite Words:

1. Asterisk: Not only is the word "asterisk" extremely harsh sounding, it is also somewhat fussy to pronounce. To say nothing of the fact that it contains the words "ass" and "risk", which are rarely good in combination form.

2. Hoot: While acceptable in reference to the sound made by an owl, in every other context the word "hoot" is simply annoying and sounds dumb. The person saying it sounds like a hillbilly, and you feel embarrassed to be in the company of someone who sounds like a hillbilly. I assume it is a derivation of the word "hootenanny" meant to indicate that something or other was "fun" or "like a party". But if the event you attended was held anywhere other than in a barn or a parking lot, you are doing your hosts a disservice by describing their event as a "hoot". Buy yourself a Thesaurus.

3. Charlatan: The word "charlatan" doesn't even sound like a real word. It sounds like somebody just made it up.

4. Fibroid: There's no way around it, the word "fibroid" sounds disgusting. While medical personnel might very well understand a "fibroid" to be the benign uterine growth that it actually is, for the rest of us it still sounds like one of those gnarly clumps of hair, dust, dead insects, toenail clippings and fecal material moldering in the corner behind the toilet of a cheap motel. So by all means, tell me I have a benign tumor, but please don't use the word "fibroid".

5. Weltanschauung: Not only is it difficult to pronounce (or even say with a straight face), it is actually impossible to use the word "weltanschauung" without sounding like a complete ass. In fact, my fully formed, philosophical view of the word is that the people who use it are pretentious.

Well, Dear Diary, as you know, I could go on – and on. But let's call it a night. Except I just want to point out a few of my other favorite words: Quark, Aplomb, Prehensile, Elucidate, Miasma and Anathema. Okay. Now I can go to bed.
Goodnight.
P.S. Confirmed everybody's still on for Tuesday night. Dinner for twelve.

55. SURPRISE!

Tuesday, August 9

Dear Diary:

Unlike me, Martin loves surprises. I know. It's weird. How my big, strong, intellectual, rational man can be such a baby about his birthday doesn't make sense. I blame Camilla.
 Anyway, for whatever reason, every August 9th I have to somehow "do it up big".
 It starts from the moment we wake up. I have to pretend I don't remember it's his birthday and let him pretend he doesn't remember it's his birthday. If I make the mistake of rolling over and saying, "Happy Birthday, honey," I will have ruined his day. I will have spoiled the surprise. I'm not even sure how such a smart man convinces himself, year after year, that nothing is going on - which is what he would have to do in order to actually be surprised. It has to be an act; a ritual that he wants played out to satisfy his inner child. Whatever.
 So we spend most of the day doing what we do every other day, until about five o'clock. That's when I complain that I've forgotten to take meat out of the freezer and insist that I just don't feel like cooking tonight. I let him suggest we can "go out for a bite", which he always does with a completely straight face, then I agree and say something along the lines of, "That sounds good. Why don't we go to La Roma? I feel like Italian." Italian food is Martin's favorite. La Roma is Martin's favorite upscale Italian restaurant. Not surprisingly, he agrees. "I'll call." I say.
 "The reservation's for 7:30," I shout down to him before stepping into the shower. Yes, I still shower before going out for dinner. Even I wouldn't set foot in La Roma without getting dressed up. Again, not sure how he manages the pretense of believing we could get a reservation at La Roma on such short notice - even on a Tuesday night. Never underestimate the power of denial.
 Luckily, I have kept a good black dress from my former life in my closet for such an occasion (or a funeral). And, with the help of a new pair of Spanx I bought last week, I can still stuff myself into it.
 As we drive up to La Roma Martin doesn't appear to notice any

of the neighbors' cars that are quite blatantly lining the street; not even Charles's quite distinctive Jaguar. Hmm.

When we open the door to the restaurant all our friends and neighbors stand up from our table for twelve and, holding their glasses of champagne up to toast Martin, simultaneously yell "Surprise!"

I'm always a little taken aback at how genuinely surprised Martin appears to be - every year. And I have come to the conclusion that he has to be one of two things. Either he has missed his calling as a great actor, or he genuinely is a little thick. I may never know, but neither is less unsettling than the other.

Well, to make a long story short, an appropriate amount of celebrating was enjoyed by all and Martin was truly pleased with his birthday surprise - especially when we got home. I know what you're thinking - but I meant when he opened the laundry room door and, with thanks to Tony for delivering it while we were out, discovered a new arc welder with a great big blue bow on it.

Until next year, Happy Birthday, my wonderfully strange husband.

Goodnight, Dear Diary.

56. TWILIGHT ZONE

Friday, August 12

Dear Diary:

It all started innocently enough. It could have been an episode of something on Netflix where I didn't want to be left hanging, or simply that I failed to press the "off" button before twenty seconds ticked by and I was instantly launched into the next episode. Maybe it was that extra cup of tea that kept me awake. I suppose it's even possible that not doing anything most days and knowing there's no real reason to get up in the morning have conspired to alter my need for sleep and my sleeping pattern. I don't know that I can point my finger to any one cause but, for whatever reason, I now find myself staying awake until 4:30 a.m. and sleeping in until around noon.

    Needless to say, I am now in the guest room. Which actually exacerbates the problem. Now there are no limits. I have paused Netflix at 3:00 a.m., gotten out of bed, made my way to the kitchen, prepared a meal for myself, eaten it, gone back to bed, and a half-hour later tiptoed down to the freezer for an ice-cream bar.

    Although my original strategy with Martin was to suggest that I might be "sleep-eating", apparently that diagnosis isn't supportable by the evidence.

    But here's the thing, not only am I not sure how to break the pattern, I'm not entirely convinced I want to.

    I feel like I have been very gradually drawn into a parallel universe where I'm living the negative image of my former life. It's kind of weirdly cool - sort of like that feeling I remember from university days when we'd stay up all night after our exams.

    In addition to being the soft glow in the sky when the sun is below the horizon, "twilight" is also a state of obscurity or ambiguity. I am now officially living in *The Twilight Zone*.

    Hmm. Must check to see if they have that on Netflix.
    Goodnight, Dear Diary.

57. OLD DOG. NEW TRICKS.

Monday, August 15

Dear Diary:

As embarrassing as it is to admit, I have only just today realized that, much like human tableware, pet dishes need to be cleaned after every meal.

Although I might have had a sort-of legitimate excuse for choosing to ignore the scummy buildup when I was working, I can't really use that anymore. I mean let's get real; I've been retired for nearly seven months.

While I have always thoroughly cleaned Mr. Boogie's dishes daily, I think I used to convince myself that dogs and cats are so over-exposed to germs of every nature and kind outdoors, at the dog park and in the litter box, that the likelihood of them being seriously harmed by their dishes being less than pristine was pretty low.

But today, for some reason, maybe because I still had my glasses on when I started to fill Lucy's dish, I was actually horrified to realize that I was about to scoop her not inexpensive, grain-free, fully balanced dinner into what was quite obviously nothing short of a Petri dish.

What is wrong with me? How could I have spent decades ignoring basic hygiene for my beloved pets? Poor Miloup died of cancer of the jaw. Did I cause that? And what about sweet Xena - did she contract Hemangiosarcoma from her scummy food dishes? What am I - crazy?

I guess the truth is that very smart people can be very stupid in some ways. It's kind of like the time when my girlfriends and I went on vacation after Law School and were sitting around engaged in the whole bath vs. shower controversy. Okay, so it never was an actual controversy, but having just graduated from Law School - well, there isn't much a bunch of lawyers won't turn into a debate. Anyway, I still remember telling my friend Caroline that I would agree with her about the shower being better, except for that shocking first blast of cold water that's been stored up in the hose. She gave me one of those looks. It's quite distinguishable from the "Well, you got me there!" look. The curled upper lip and scrunched up nose give it away. It's more the "What kind of a dumb-ass are you?" look. We've all seen it. All of us. The look was followed by the words, "Don't you let the water run for a minute before you get in?" The words were spoken extremely slowly and distinctly with the same inflection you use with your "slow" cousin. My first thought was, "What kind of a dumb-ass am I?" I was twenty-four years old. It had literally never even occurred to me to let the water run for a minute before I got in the shower. My head was spinning. How did Caroline know about this? Had somebody taught it to her? Had she dreamed it up all on her own? Was she gifted? Was I stupid? How did I ever get into Law School? Does everybody else know about this?

There was only one other time in my life when I experienced that same level of self-doubt. The following year when I was articling at a law firm out of town, Sarah had come to stay in my apartment with me for a while. I had been living in the apartment for six months. After washing a load of her laundry in my private laundry "closet" she turned to me and said, "Yech! When was the last time you cleaned out the filter in the washing machine?" I wanted to say, "What filter?" but caught myself. Instead, I muttered, "Sorry about that," hoping she would attribute the filthy filter to a lapse in memory and not a complete lack of knowledge. How could I not know that washing machines in those days had filters that you were supposed to clean out? I felt dirty. Dirty and stupid. Like I had been adopted after everybody else had been given the top-secret washing machine instructions. Who was supposed to be in charge of relaying that information, anyway? And why had it been kept from me? I felt like the eleven-year-old kid who only realized half way through third period that she had put her T-shirt on inside out and backwards (okay, that was me too).

All of that to say that when I looked at Lucy's slimy food dish I knew I had to start taking better care of her; that from this moment forward I would take every possible precaution to keep her healthy. When she dies, it's not going to be because I was too stupid to own a pet. I may have come late to the table, but at least I was going to figure this out all on my own. No humiliating stage whispers from guests looking sideways at my pets' dinner dishes. "Was she raised by wolves?" "I thought she was smart!" "What is the matter with her?" No way. I was going to nip this thing in the bud (if thirty years of negligent pet ownership could be called "the bud").

So now, every time Lucy and Twink eat or drink they are doing it out of dishes that have been soaked in boiling water and vinegar and scrubbed with soap, rinsed and dried. I now treat washing their dishes with the gravitas of a nuclear meltdown cleanup operation. I may not have a job any more, but I do have responsibilities. Serious responsibilities.

Still, self-doubt can do a real number on your confidence, and I can't help but wonder if there are other basic things that I either never learned or am doing wrong. Do I brush "up and down" or "back and forth"? I'm not really sure any more. Has Martin been correct all these years - there really is a "right" way to replace the roll of toilet paper? Do you really "have" to wait for the oven to reach the right temperature? Are you actually "supposed" to use the parking break? Does everybody else always unplug the TV during a thunderstorm? Life can be so complicated.

Hmm. Unsettling. Think I'll go brush my teeth up and down and back and forth - just to be sure.

Goodnight, Dear Diary.

58. SO IT HAS COME TO THIS …

Thursday, August 18

Dear Diary:

We went to the doctor today to get the results of some blood tests.
    I am the one who insisted we go in the first place because I wanted Martin to start getting his prostate checked. I really only went along as a means of getting him to agree to go.
    Of course all of Martin's test results were perfect. I, on the other hand, apparently have low B12 and should start taking supplements.
    Great. Last year they suggested I start taking Vitamin D supplements. Add the B12 to that and the hormone replacement therapy, and now there's no sensible alternative but to set myself up with a seven-day pill organizer.
    Yes, it has come to this.
    Think I'll order one on line. There's no way I'm going to risk running into Charles at Walmart while I'm in the process of buying a pill organizer. I'd rather be the one wearing the blue vest.
    Goodnight, Dear Diary. I have to go take my medicine.

59. PILLEMMA

Monday, August 22

Dear Diary:

My pill organizer arrived today.

    I'm not sure if I'm the only one who does this but, sometimes when I'm bummed out I will try to find the one thing that is most likely to take my bad mood and turn it into a death spiral of anxiety, depression and self-loathing.

    Of course there are those other people who always prefer to remain "chipper" (I hate that word) no matter what. "Well, tomorrow's another day." "Things could be a lot worse." "I really have so much to be thankful for."

    Well, every cloud does not have a silver lining. And I not only think it's as healthy to allow myself to feel the negative emotions as it is to feel the positive ones, I actually go out of my way on occasion to really let the negativity sink into my gut and screw with my head - for a while. I don't always want to put bad things "out of my mind". There are times when I just need to feel the misery, taste it in the back of my throat and let it cling to my soul like dog poop on hiking boots.

    And for some reason, the arrival this morning of the seven-day pill organizer brought me to that place. Today was a turning point of some sort. I felt my age. There was no turning back the hands of time. Time…aah, I knew just the thing.

    If you have never actually sat down and listened to the words of the 1973 song *Time* by Pink Floyd, a word of caution. While perfectly suitable for my needs today, if you are over the age of nineteen and have ever been prescribed medication to help you "get through the day", then please do yourself a favor and move on to the next entry.

    For those of you who are a tad more contemplative, well balanced and less faint of heart, go ahead. Listen to *Time*. And as you are listening, feel free to ask yourselves: Have you "missed the starting gun"? Are you "hanging on in quiet desperation"? Do you feel like "the song is over"? Or like you thought you "had something more to say"?

    Feeling bummed yet? I know. Works like a charm. Takes you

right to that sweet spot between ambivalent and suicidal.

Now go and do a Sudoku or put on some dancing music. Snap out of it!

Goodnight, Dear Diary.

60. MASTERMIND

Wednesday, August 24

Dear Diary:

The power of words never ceases to amaze me.

And it would behoove persons in certain circumstances to be aware of the effect their word choices can have. Which is to say, a word choice can significantly alter the outcome of an exchange you might be contemplating with someone. So if manipulation is your goal, you should consider very carefully what it is you want to say. And if your spidey senses ever tell you someone's words are being used to elicit a specific reaction from you, you are probably correct.

Take police interrogations, just as an example. The same person who will vehemently deny being the "ringleader" of a heinous criminal activity may prove surprisingly reluctant to deny being the "Mastermind" of the exact same activity. Why? Human nature, pure and simple.

You see, "ringleader", although it contains the word "leader", is strongly suggestive of hooliganism or hijinks, which smack of pettiness, delinquency and possibly general stupidity. On principle alone, even an actual "ringleader" is simply never going to want to admit to being a "ringleader".

An accusation of being a "Mastermind", on the other hand, despite the potentially disadvantageous consequences of an admission, has just a hint of a compliment about it, suggesting to the perpetrator an element of respect for him and a concession to his authority, decisiveness and intellectual horsepower. This, at a subconscious level, almost demands his acquiescence to your assessment. "Okay, okay, you got me. Yes. I am the Mastermind." Note: This is why lawyers don't want their clients to ever say anything to the police. Also Note: This is why idiots sometimes find themselves in the position of having "confessed" to any number of dastardly undertakings of which they are entirely innocent.

The ego is a strange creature, and it can feed on the most unlikely morsels. Make no mistake; you don't have to be the subject of a police interrogation to fall prey to the very same tactics. Subconscious responses to word choices are, in fact, the only reason a woman finds herself cooking meals every day for fifty or sixty years for a perfectly healthy man. Based on little more than what appear to be a series of spontaneous and perfectly innocent remarks like, "This is really good," or "Judith's a great cook," a woman can find herself thinking, "I hope he likes this," as she pours over a recipe for the fifteen thousandth meal she is about to prepare, when the far more logical thought would quite clearly be, "Why the hell isn't he the one trying to figure out how to cook gobo root?"

So if you find yourself feeling complimented about anything, no matter how mundane it may seem at the time, think long and hard about why. And maybe start appreciating your critics - they don't usually want (or get) anything from you.

Goodnight, Dear Diary.

61. DREAM MAKER

Sunday, August 28

Dear Diary:

Some people believe that dreams can predict the future, but I have to say that I don't see much evidence that they can even accurately portray the present.

    Here's my problem. All our dreams come from our own brains, right? So tell me then how these four things are even possible:

    1. People you have never seen before can appear in your dreams. I don't mean people you have never met before, I mean people who are not now and never have been alive on earth. Even in books or paintings. Your brain has made them up out of thin air. If I can't draw a human face, the skills for which are no doubt controlled by my brain, how can my brain draw a human face and body and then animate it in my dreams? More to the point, if my brain can conceive of and create human faces and bodies and animate them, then why can't I draw?

    2. In day-to-day life, it is your brain that "alerts" you when something is "not right". It could be a green cow, an upside down street sign or a bad toupee. But the same brain that alerts you to such mundane anomalies doesn't seem to have any problem when, in a dream, wearing only your underwear, you step out onto your back deck and find yourself in the middle of a shopping mall full of people who are then, without the benefit of any ascertainable means of transportation, instantly in a giant desert walking rabbits on leashes towards a spaceship poorly disguised as an ocean liner. How is it that the same brain that, when you are awake, says "What's wrong with this picture?" when you see a couple wearing matching outfits, has absolutely no problem, in a dream state, with your dead father sitting at the dinner table carrying on an animated conversation and looking quizzically at you every time you try to gently "remind" him that he is dead? Why doesn't it jolt you awake the very second you have created something that cannot possibly exist in reality? On the contrary, your brain appears to have no issue with producing countless nonsensical, if not downright impossible, images and situations without so much as a whiff of incredulity. "Of course you

are the most beautiful seventeen-year-old girl in the world caught in a downpour on a lonely road in the middle of Paris when Idris Elba swoops down in his private jet to rescue you." Your brain doesn't intercede during that particular creation process and say, "C'mon. When are you ever going to be in Paris?" Or how about when you dream that aliens abduct you from the Nobel Peace Prize ceremony being held in your honor? Does your brain even try to nudge you back to reality? "You know you work at Denny's, right?" No it does not. Apparently, your sleeping brain believes that situation is "totally doable." In fact, your brain allows any number of incongruous scenarios to play out without sending you one single alert that something is "not right".

3. I also want to know how it is that you can surprise yourself in a dream. How can one part of your dreaming brain "not know" that if you turn that corner up ahead as your are sauntering blithely down an avenue, another part of your brain has your Grade Nine boyfriend standing there waiting to "bump into" you? You have created the entire scenario in your one brain. You have set yourself up to "be surprised" - and you are. How is that possible? Is the part of your brain that has the boyfriend hiding around the corner not in touch with the part of your brain that has you strolling down the avenue?

4. Although related to number three above, the final example really deserves a category all its own. A surprise is one thing; a night terror is quite another, and even more inexplicable. You can be picking flowers in a sunny meadow and humming church hymns in your dream when a horrifying monster with a cavernous, slime and blood-filled maw rises out of the ground in front of you and starts clawing at your face - all without so much as a hint to the part of you that is lollygagging in the meadow that anything might be amiss. How can one part of your brain not have the remotest clue what some other part of your brain is up to when, in real life, it could actually induce a heart attack? How is it that your brain can be craftily creating an impending horror at the same time that it is lulling you into tranquility? Your brain is doing all of this. All of it.

I don't get it. I just don't get it. As if real life doesn't have enough mysteries of its own, why do our brains mess with us like this? Usually when we're asleep - but not always. And what's really scary is that we rely on these organs to run our entire lives, from motor control and hormone secretion, to motivation, memory, emotions and bodily functions. Our brains are in control. Do they have too much power? Maybe.

Perhaps "listen to your heart and not your head" isn't such bad advice after all.

Well, must be off to let my brain "do its thing". No telling what it has in store for me tonight.

Goodnight, Dear Diary. Hello Idris Elba.

62. SPOT CLEANING

Thursday, September 1

Dear Diary:

In the incredible, revolving, mutant night warrior world of cleaning protocols, I believe I may have finally come up with a solution to my inability to actually implement any of my previous plans.

In my defense, they all tended to be rather complex, time-consuming and - well, boring. I think it's fair to say that I'm just not a housekeeper at heart. The truth is, I don't really care enough about living in perfect surroundings or what anybody else might think if the "finger test" on the top of my picture frames comes back "negative". Big deal. So what. I concede. Everybody else is a better housekeeper than I am. Can we move on?

When I go into someone else's house and everything is sparkling and perfect, I have to say that my first thought is never "Wow! You are an awesome housekeeper!" No, my first thought is more likely "I guess this is one of those houses where we have to take our shoes off." Upon the heels of which my second thought is usually, "Shit. I knew I should have worn my good socks."

Anyway, in my bid to maintain "sensible" status for our house, I think I've finally hit the nail on the head. Of course I do always have a clean kitchen - and the toilet bowls and sinks are kept in reasonable check - it's just the rest of the house that continues to be problematic. My solution? Well, I remembered the old days, when my Mom used to do everything in her power to avoid having to spend money at the drycleaner's. My Mom would "spot clean" Dad's suits and ties, her dresses and jackets and all the kids' coats. And it occurred to me that there was no reason why I couldn't apply that same technique to our entire house.

So here's what I do. If I "happen to notice" a thick layer of dust on something, I wipe it off. It can be a tabletop, light fixture, leather chair, windowsill, bed frame, computer screen or favorite knick-knack. Whatever it is, if the sunlight exposes an unacceptable level of dirt, I am on it like white on rice. Simple. And it's usually no more than about thirty seconds of work. The real secret to this method is to not trouble yourself with the obvious conclusions and rote reflexes that will take you to that place where you'll assume if one shelf on the buffet is in need of attention, the other three shelves must also be in need of attention. Under no circumstances should you allow yourself to go hunting for dirt and dust. That's a game you cannot win. That's the kind of thinking that will drag you back down into the housecleaning rabbit hole, make you miserable and totally defeat the whole purpose of "spot cleaning". Besides, who knows, maybe you cleaned one of those other shelves a couple of days ago. And therein lies the beauty of "spot cleaning". Denial.

Of course the "spot cleaning" rules do go out the window when we've invited people over. I'm not an animal.

Goodnight, Dear Diary. I'll just stick you back on the night table now ... oh. Damn. Is that dust?

63. OLDER VS. OLD

Sunday, September 4

Dear Diary:

Now that I'm sixty, I find myself wondering at times where I "fit" in life.

Can I still get away with thinking of myself as middle-aged? Aye, there's the rub. I remember very well the day I turned forty-five and Martin made a point of informing me that I was now officially middle-aged. "Oh my God! Don't ever say that again!" But life goes on - if you're lucky - and eventually we reach another slot into which we are pushed, kicking and screaming, based solely on the date of our birth. While Wikipedia says that I am middle-aged until I reach sixty-five, the hardware store considers me to be a "senior" now that I've reached sixty.

It's all very confusing - and depressing. And although it can be nice to get discounts and qualify for certain pensions, I think what really bothers me most is wondering whether or not people actually think of me as old. It's not that I see myself as old, but you don't need to look too far to realize that people are not really only as old as they feel. I'm very well aware of the fact that going around claiming to not feel old doesn't make me young again - or even "less old".

After some soul-searching and considerable thought, I have concluded that maybe I fit into a new category. Maybe I am not so much actually old now, as I'm just "older". Of course by "older" I don't mean older than old, I mean older than middle-aged, somewhere between middle-aged and old. I know it's a fine line that I'm drawing, but I could live with being thought of as merely "older".

All that is lacking is a set of useful criteria for assessing what distinguishes the old from those who are merely "older" (like me). For those who may come after me and be pondering this very same question, I have therefore taken the liberty of setting out what I believe to be the seven most significant criteria to use when assessing where you fit. Are you old, or just "older"?

1. Farting In Public: Only one of you can get away with farting in public. Or, as my Mom still calls it, "making a noise". People will openly display disgust when the merely "older" fart in public,

possibly subjecting them to any number of forms of humiliation (vigorous hand fanning, wrinkling their noses, holding their breath in an exaggerated fashion or making rude comments). The old, on the other hand, tend to elicit little more than a giggle or a sympathetic smile from the public, if that. Generally, people will treat farting by the old as if it didn't even happen, in much the same way that the old tend to treat it themselves. So if you are farting in public and nobody is saying or doing anything - sorry, my friend, you fall into the old category. But as you can see, it does come with certain perks.

2. Lameness: Here's where the merely "older" have the advantage over the old. I know. Surprising, isn't it? If people are treating you with sympathy and going out of their way to accommodate and help you, you are merely "older". For the truly old, on the other hand, lameness to one degree or another is almost a given. "Oh great. Does Granny really have to come shopping with us? She's so slow." Or, "I'm not going to bother inviting Uncle Jim for Thanksgiving this year - he could hardly make it up the front steps last year." For the old, lameness is treated more like a tiresome personality trait than a physical condition. Any real sympathy has long since faded. Why? Because they know you're never going to improve! They know that it's only going to go downhill from here on in! They're tired of always having to help you up the stairs or into the bathroom. They're fed up with escorting you at a snail's pace, no matter what the weather, to and from the car that brought you. And you never bring your own umbrella. If people are always half-heartedly lurching towards you with pained expressions on their faces every time you take a step - then you are old. If, on the other hand, they treat you like you have been injured and are in need of their understanding and assistance, then you are merely "older". People tend to be very kind to someone who needs help, as long as the affliction is understood to be temporary. If friends show up at your door with prepared meals for your family, then you are "older". If your family leaves a "meals on wheels" brochure on your coffee table - I hate to be the one to have to tell you this - but you are old.

3. Forgetfulness: Have you ever forgotten someone's name, lost your car keys or caught yourself saying to the person next to you, "What's that word again? You know. For that thing…" Congratulations, you are merely "older". Now try to recall if you have ever heard anyone say any of these things to you:

"It's me, Mom. Carla. Your daughter."
"Yes you have been here before, Dad. You live here."
"No, Uncle Raymond isn't coming. He died eight years ago."
"Hello ma'am. It's the superintendent. Is there water running in your apartment?"
"This is 9-1-1. What is your emergency?"
If you have heard two or more of those statements in the past twelve months, you are old. If you simply can't remember whether or not you have heard two or more of those statements in the past twelve months, then you are actually really old.

4. Fashion: If people tell you (usually from a distance) every time they see you how nice you look, even when your hair hasn't been washed for two weeks, your blouse has food stains on it from last Christmas, your shoes don't match or you are wearing your underwear on top of your pants, you are old. If people never compliment you any more on your appearance no matter how much effort you have put in or how new or expensive your outfit is, then you are merely "older". Hurray. If people start complimenting you on your jewelry, you are old. What they are really doing is getting their dibs in. That's right. Don't kid yourself. If people are refusing pieces of your jewelry because it isn't "their style", you are merely "older", and your kids are ungrateful. Trust me. It'll come back in style one of these days and they'll all be clamoring for it when you are old.

5. Face Food: Has anybody ever said to you, "There's a little something on your … yeah … right there"? If so, you are only "older". If, on the other hand, you have glanced at yourself in the mirror before getting ready for bed and found birthday cake crusted on your chin and red wine dribbled down your shirt, all of which have been there since you attended your daughter's party three hours ago, then you are old. When you are merely "older", people still treat you as if you are a person; "one of them", if you will. They will say or do something when you have food on your face or spill spaghetti sauce on your clothes. They may even reach over and try to help you clean it off. But people don't want to touch the old. In an ironic twist on "finders keepers", nobody wants to be the one who "finds" the food on your face or the drink spilled all over your sweater when you are old because they don't want to be the one who has to clean you up. Why? A number of reasons. First of all, there is every

possibility that between your bad eyesight, failing memory, shaky hands, long fingernails and poor balance, you are covered in ecoli. Secondly, it's not unheard of for a cloud of weird smells to hover over you. Not unlike a cake of lavender soap soaked in urine. Possibly with a top note of fart that wasn't just a fart. And finally, people simply don't want to get "old" all over them. There's a reason they sit you at the head of the table. It's because nobody wants to sit beside you.

 6. Loud Voices: Have you noticed lately that, despite the fact there is nothing wrong with your hearing, whenever people say something to you they stare directly into your eyes, raise their voices and speak unnaturally slowly? Then you are old. For those of us who are merely "older", people do almost the exact opposite. So maybe just smile to yourself when people mumble something incomprehensible in response to your questions without even looking at you. They obviously don't think of you as old. You still got it, baby.

 7. Medical Treatment: If medical personnel have ever called you "dear", you are old. If the doctor appears ambivalent about ordering "another test", you are old. If the doctor addresses every question to someone else in the room, you are old. This last one should be self-explanatory, but here goes - if medical personnel ever ask, "Do you know what a DNR is?" it doesn't really matter any more where you fit.

 If these tips on figuring out whether or not you are truly old yet can help just one person hold their head up through the next family dinner, my effort will have been worth it.

 Goodnight, Dear Diary.

64. OOH ... SPARKLES!

Wednesday, September 7

Dear Diary:

I know it has been eight months since I retired, but there are still those days when I feel like my life has been stripped of all meaning.

Today was another one of those days. Sure there were things I probably should have been doing. I just didn't want to do them. It was a little bit like when you're supposed to be studying for an exam but will use almost any excuse to avoid sitting at your desk. "Wow, those baseboards are dirty! I better get on that!"

So, rather than vacuum the house or do yet another load of laundry, I decided to wander around the mall. Do you know that up until today I had never been in a craft store in my life? Crazy, right?

Well, I happened to glance into the craft store window at the mall as I was walking past, and I saw giant containers filled with beautiful sparkles. Although I've never been a fan of sparkles (or frills or bows) on clothing or in people's hair, the sun must have been hitting the jars just right, because those sparkles looked like someone had scooped up the fairy dust from an iridescent rainbow that had fallen to earth. They were mesmerizing. Unable to pull myself away, I stepped inside.

Everywhere I looked was a shelf full of wondrous things I had never seen before, each more fascinating than the last. There were tiny cake and candy molds, cookie cutters shaped like flowers, jars of colored icing, cake decorations, dessert stands, fancy foil wrap, cute little treat boxes, metallic crinkle and party decorations. I fondled every single item like a starving person in a grocery store.

There were glass, crystal and metallic beads and charms of every color, shape and size. There were jewelry designing kits, glitter glues, giant wooden letters, fabric, wool, colored tape and art supplies.

There were ribbons; there were bows. There were wedding supplies, picture frames, scented candles and floating candles. There were lanterns, wreaths, reindeer moss, dried flowers, floral sprays and colored lights.

It was Halloween, Christmas, a birthday party, wedding celebration and Fun Fair all rolled into one. It was amazing. Not the way people say something is "amazing" when it actually falls quite short of that. This was really startlingly impressive, and left me filled with wonder.

I felt like a whole new world of possibilities had opened up. My head was spinning. My imagination went wild:

...I could start making homemade chocolates and create beautiful, fancy gift boxes for Christmas. Or make little animal cookies all decorated by hand to give out at the Children's Hospital. Our front door would look so beautiful with a Harvest Wreath for Thanksgiving. And what about the state of decrepitude of our sad, old Christmas wreath? I could make us a new one! Why, I could even start making ornaments for our Christmas tree. Maybe send boxes of handmade ornaments to Grace and Joey. It's never too soon to start your ornament collection.

And perhaps I should learn how to knit. There's going to be a grandchild coming at some point. OMG, I almost forgot. Halloween's just around the corner. Wouldn't the neighborhood kids get a kick out of homemade cupcakes hand decorated with little goblins and pumpkins and witches? That would be so adorable. Who wants another chocolate bar anyway? Oh, this is going to be fun!

I wonder if Tony and Jessica are going to get married? I could volunteer to be their wedding planner. I have to call Sophie and tell her. Just wait 'til they see all this cute stuff! This is so exciting!

Mind you, I've also always wondered whether or not I could paint. I mean, I know I can't draw, but maybe I could paint. Oh great, they have easels. Perfect. No time like the present. Hmm. Do I go with watercolors, oils, pastels or acrylics? Why not try them all...

Two hours after entering the store the fog started to lift. I was inching a cart packed with merchandise through the checkout line. I stopped, looked down at the overloaded cart and froze. What was all this stuff? There were baking supplies, art supplies, sprays of flowers and greenery. There were plastic pumpkins, decals, boxes of beads and tiny elf lights. There was a cardboard turkey. But what really caught my attention was the giant jar of rainbow-colored sparkles in the middle of the cart. I picked it up and looked at it. Carefully. I held it up to the light. It seemed to have lost some of its shimmer. Hmm. Maybe it wasn't quite as special as it had seemed in the window.

I poked at everything in the cart. It was starting to look more like the one dollar grab box left over at the end of a garage sale. And it looked like making anything out of it all would boil down to a considerable amount of work. Who's going to do the vacuuming?

Suddenly I felt very tired. I stepped away from the cart and headed out the door.

And as I walked towards my car I realized that there was probably a very good reason I had never been inside a craft store before. Sure, my self-awareness might have been suspended for a couple of hours today, but the truth is - I'm just not very crafty.

I think I'll put my experience today down to the same phenomenon that makes a person who reads a good book briefly toy with the notion that they could actually be a writer.

Note to self: Remember to call Sophie tomorrow and tell her to ignore that voicemail message.

Goodnight, Dear Diary.

65. JUST WHEN YOU THOUGHT YOU WERE OUT

Tuesday, September 13

Dear Diary

Mom called this morning. She "forgot" she had to get an x-ray done this afternoon. Mom lives an hour and a half from me. Mom doesn't drive.

Here's the thing about retirement. It's not entirely dissimilar from purchasing a pickup truck. Although both symbolize freedom, ironically, both actually set you up as the "go to" person for all your family and friends. "Fred's got that new pickup. He can help us move." Or, "Don't worry about the weather, dear. Jane's retired. She can take us to the dentist." It is always assumed that you have nothing better to do.

And as much empathy as I might have for the guy with the new pickup, unless he has like a million friends, at least people aren't going to ask him to move, haul or tow crap several times a week.

For retirees, on the other hand, having old parents who are still alive and within driving distance is the equivalent of having a million friends. Except that they're not your friends. You might not even like them. If you had any choice they might not even be acquaintances. You can say "no" to a friend. You cannot say "no" to your old parents. You just end up looking and feeling like a total jerk. "Did you know poor Agnes had to miss her biopsy appointment? Barbara refused to take her to the hospital."

If you thought your parents were tiresome when you were working, take my advice. When you retire, move away. Move far away. Move so far away that you would have to get on an airplane to visit them. The smart kids in the family have already put as much distance as possible between the parents and themselves long before they hit retirement age.

But have you ever noticed how it is always the kids who live outside the "responsibility perimeter" who have the most advice on what the parents need and what you should be doing for them? Uncanny, isn't it? And they're sneaky about it - they don't call you and ask you first. They call the parents and tell them about all the products they really ought to try and the stuff they need or should think about having done or tested. Thanks a bunch, Fred. But do the parents appreciate what you do? On the contrary, if Fred calls once every four weeks they're nearly beside themselves with joy and can't stop talking about how wonderful he is - and what great advice he's always giving them. If, on the other hand, after dragging her to five different appointments in a month you actually can't take your Mom to the hairdresser today because you are having surgery, then your name is mud.

It's really hard to be proactive about your new life when you're literally on call 24/7. Just when you thought you were going to finally have some personal freedom, parents can pull you back into their frenzied world of rush-hour traffic, emergency hospital admissions, dental appointments, visits with distant cousins and shopping expeditions. My Mom is obviously not paying attention to those TV commercials where old people are saying, "I don't want to be a burden to my kids."

Of course Sarah helps too, but we could definitely use more staff. It's almost worse that a full-time job, because it's event-driven and subject to laws of randomness. At least with my job there were specific working hours - and holidays. There are no holidays from your parents needs. They can and do occur at any time on any given day.

Thank God Camilla and Aksel don't rely on us for very much - yet.

Goodnight, Dear Diary. (...Love you, Mom).

66. NAPPING INJURIES

Friday, September 16

Dear Diary:

It used to be that a nap was a few stolen mid-afternoon moments in our giant armchair when my eyes had grown heavy with reading, or twenty minutes of repose before the timer on the stove signaled the potatoes were done. It could even have been a brief interlude between cleaning up the kitchen after dinner and putting the kettle on for tea. That was then.

Now, napping has taken on a life all its own. It is both entirely different in nature, and has assumed entirely different proportions. What were once probably best described as short, light sleeps or states of relaxation and drowsiness are now two to three-hour periods of unconsciousness. Way beyond "power-napping" or even "extreme napping", Martin tells me that if it weren't for the snoring (which I'm pretty sure he's making up) he would think I had fallen into a coma.

It's fair to say that a significant portion of my day is now consumed by napping which, in turn, has been wreaking havoc with my whole sleep-wake pattern.

But the worst side effect of prolonged napping during the day has been that I seem to have sustained more injuries in the last seven months than in the previous fifty-nine years. While evidence of any causal connection between napping and my injuries may be more circumstantial than direct, when I wake up on the couch with a crick in my neck or stiff knee I don't see how it could reasonably be attributed to anything else.

And if I hadn't been napping on the couch, chances are that when I flailed my arm out in my sleep I wouldn't have smashed the back of my hand into the tall ceramic lamp that used to sit on the sofa table behind the couch, giving myself a bad bruise that turned black and blue and didn't go away for two weeks.

Likewise, I have twisted my back just trying to get up off the couch. None of these things happen in bed, so I can only conclude that there is some relationship between these injuries and napping.

Today was the worst. I was woken up from my nap by the

sound of the telephone ringing. Startled, I sprang up off the sofa to grab the telephone, but was overcome by a dizzy spell. When I tried to balance myself, my right knee locked and I stubbed my left toe on the iron leg of the glass coffee table. When I raised my left foot up to ease the searing pain, my whole body was thrown completely off balance, I fell sideways into the glass table top, and cracked my elbow and the side of my head. But the sheer momentum of the fall kept my body moving forward, so that I rolled and slid across the sharp iron corner of the table and down onto the floor, badly scraping my rib cage and face. It would appear that napping is more dangerous than leaping from moving yachts.

In fact, napping has become such a perilous pastime that it wouldn't surprise me at all to read in the Obituaries one of these days that someone had "died napping". I don't mean, died "while" napping, as in passed away in their sleep while taking a nap (like everybody doesn't want to die "while" napping). No, I mean that the physical act of napping is going to actually kill somebody one of these days.

Which reminds me, while I'm on the subject of Obituaries, there was one in this morning's paper where a family described their ninety-year-old relative as having "died suddenly". I have to say, if your family member has "shuffled off this mortal coil" at the age of ninety, there are literally no circumstances in which that death can be described as "sudden". I don't care if your granny was struck by lightning at the age of ninety, she cannot be described as having died "suddenly". If a lightning bolt kills you at the age of ninety, it just means that the world has taken ninety years to come up with a way to finally get rid of you. It had been trying to do precisely that since the day you were born. The fact that it ultimately had to resort to using a lightning bolt just means that you spent ninety years avoiding every other conceivable means of complying with the laws of mortality. Congratulations should be in order. But your death was by no means "sudden".

Well, I'm still aching all over and starting to feel sleepy. Think I'll take advantage of that and try to get some real sleep.

Goodnight, Dear Diary.

67. METAMORPHOSIS

Monday, September 19

Dear Diary:

Nobody ever described me as a social butterfly. Ever. While I do "socialize" and can be "sociable", I just don't often meet people who are so fascinating to me that I feel like I really need to get to know them better or be their friend.

I might even go so far as to say that, when I was working, I always made a point of avoiding friendships with co-workers and clients. When you're being paid to provide legal advice, you don't want personal relationships to compromise your advice in any way. Call me a purist, but I never gave legal advice based on anything other than the law. My advice was never designed to please anyone. It was never based on what anyone wanted to hear or how much I wanted anyone to like me or "approve" of my work.

Of course legal opinions also incorporate risk management and strategy advice. And I could construct legal arguments to defend my clients, prolong negotiations or "assume a position" that I knew to be ultimately untenable at law. Just because you know you won't "win" doesn't necessarily mean you have to immediately cry "uncle". But legal advice should never be a popularity contest. In fact, advice from any professional should never be a popularity contest. If your advisors are always in agreement with you, either you are the smartest person in the world (who simply didn't want to go to the bother of acquiring the necessary credentials to be licensed), or you are a megalomaniac (read "idiot"). I have known people like you. You have all been idiots.

That aside, my real point is simple. I've never been driven by a need for acceptance or approval at any level. I've never cultivated more than a few close friendships. Some people need to be liked. I don't. Or should I say, I didn't.

Something has happened to me since yesterday. It all started innocently enough. First, I received an unsolicited message from LinkedIn that appeared to suggest that a former colleague wanted me to use the web site to stay in touch. As he was one of the few people I had real respect (and time) for, I joined LinkedIn. Only hours later,

I was contacted by an old high school acquaintance through something called classmates.com. More out of curiosity than anything else, I joined that as well.

Today, I spent the entire day on Facebook. I was psychologically unable to pull myself away. I was "friending" people, "liking" everything from soap products to videos and finding myself pulled in a hundred different directions. Apparently there is a term for all of these sites. It is called "social networking".

If only I had known. Only forty-eight hours in, and already I appear to have become a "prisoner of my own device". Be warned. They are all "programmed to receive". "You can check-out any time you like, but you can never leave!" The Eagles. Forty years ahead of their time.

Goodnight, Dear Diary. I just need to post a couple of more photos…then I'm done.

68. BE KIND. REWIND.

Friday, September 23

Dear Diary:

I finally pulled myself away from Facebook today. Instead, I watched a few of my favorite movies that we had on DVD. There are some movies that just never disappoint, no matter how often you've seen them. And although certain ones were critically acclaimed, others are just so much fun to watch that anybody else's assessment is irrelevant. They are the movies that thrill me, make me laugh out loud, frighten me, make me think and touch my heart.

Best Movies Ever:
  1. *The Godfather* (1972): One of the greatest stories ever told. Superb.
  2. *The Exorcist* (1973): While most of us are pretty confident that vampires and werewolves don't exist, what makes *The Exorcist* so frightening is that, deep down, we're not entirely convinced that Satan doesn't. That's why we still can't hear *Tubular Bells* without feeling just a little bit creeped out.
  3. *Apocalypse Now* (1979): I'm not sure if anything in life, let alone the movies, inspires such mixed emotions as when Robert Duvall, who has just led a helicopter gunship napalm strike on a Vietnamese village to the accompaniment of Wagner's *Ride of the Valkyries*, says "Charlie don't surf."
  4. *Breaker Morant* (1980): You will pick a side. You may be wrong. You won't care.
  5. *Gallipoli* (1981): The essence of war. The heartbreak and moral absurdity of war. War without all the cool equipment.
  6. *The Year of Living Dangerously* (1982): Another great Australian film. A word of caution. You will never again feel like the story of how you met your partner is worth telling. "Us? Oh, we met at the dog park. Yeah. Kismet."
  7. *Ghostbusters* (1984): For pure comedy magic, "Who you gonna call?"
  8. *Back To The Future* (1985): Wonderful "feel good" movie. Everybody likes to imagine what they would do if they could time

travel. It's even great fun to watch someone else get the chance.

9. *Full Metal Jacket* (1987): Vincent D'Onofrio's performance is unforgettable. The most relatable war movie of all time.

10. *Robocop* (1987): They had me when Enforcement Droid - Series 209 wasted Kinney. That scene just never gets old.

11. *Mississippi Burning* (1988): The score alone holds you in its grip from the second it starts until the last credit has gone by. And no actor in the history of movie making has made more out of a single word that Gene Hackman when he says, "deputy".

12. *Goodfellas* (1990): If you're in the mood for an awesome gangster movie with a brilliant soundtrack and unforgettable performances, this is your movie.

13. *What About Bob* (1991): Richard Dreyfuss deserved an Academy Award for his delivery to Bill Murray of the single line, "Get out of the car!" This movie could cure clinical depression.

14. *My Cousin Vinny* (1992): Joe Pesci and Marisa Tomei are hands down the best comedy couple of all time.

15. *Reservoir Dogs* (1992): Alarmingly and unabashedly raw. You will not be able to look away.

16. *Schindler's List* (1993): As brutal as it is to watch, it is a tale that must be told. And told again. Human nature in all its complexity, from its worst to its best, is compelling portrayed in this true story of horror and of hope.

17. *Pulp Fiction* (1994): An art form all its own, this movie is like a Twinkie. It doesn't have an expiration date.

18. *Fargo* (1996): A gem. Truly, a gem. You will cringe for William H. Macy as Jerry Lundegaard, and be awed by Frances McDormand's flawlessly understated portrayal of Marge Gunderson.

19. *The Bourne Identity, Supremacy and Ultimatum* (2002, 2004, 2007): I am counting these three movies as one, because they are like potato chips. You cannot watch just one.

20. *The Departed* (2006): You will want to pick a side. You may not be able to. The A-list cast and soundtrack are the icing on an already delicious cake.

21. *Ironman* (2008): Thrilling, funny, great cast, awesome special effects. Tons of fun.

22. *Taken* (2009): There's something about Liam Neeson. Minimalist menace with well-honed credibility and unsurpassed follow-through.

Worst Movies Ever:

1. *The Enigma of Kaspar Hauser* (1974): Anyone who says that they thought this was a good movie is lying. I know. I was in the theatre when it first came out and watched everyone rise half-way out of their seats several times throughout the film, each of us hoping, "Surely this is the end. It can't possibly go on any longer." But then the film kept rolling and there were audible sighs of exasperation as we all felt we had to sit back down again, no one daring to point a finger at the "masterpiece" and say out loud what we were all thinking, "The emperor has no clothes." In short, this movie was absolutely brutal to sit through. The worst movie of all time.

There are no other movies in this list. Whenever I find a movie too bad to watch, I just turn it off. I couldn't turn Kaspar off because my date had purchased the tickets. While I suppose it isn't fair to make up a "Worst Movies Ever" list of one, you should bear in mind that I am actually quite easily amused when it comes to movies. I have watched plenty of "iffy" movies in my life, some of which I will even confess to having found mildly entertaining (*Ishtar* - I'm just saying). So you can derive some comfort from knowing that the one movie on my "Worst Movies Ever" list had to be hopelessly unwatchable.

As it turns out, I've actually bored myself sleepy just thinking about Kaspar Hauser.

Goodnight, Dear Diary.

69. "THE EAGLE HAS LANDED"

Wednesday, September 28

Dear Diary:

As I was watching Mr. Boogie today, he hopped off his swing and down into the middle of his food dish, and the phrase "The Eagle has landed" came to mind. Neil Armstrong. July 20, 1969. I remember it well.

And then I wondered to myself whether or not I am like a bird that just isn't bothering to fly. And thinking about birds made me recall the many "bird incidents" that have occurred in my life. I don't mean that I have found birds that have stunned themselves by flying into windows or injured themselves on telephone or hydro wires. Those things happen all the time. And yes, I have had my share of those stories. I am referring to events of a completely different nature, and I'm not sure what they "mean", if anything. Maybe I just tend to notice birds more than the average person, but there is little question that I have experienced my share of "interesting" bird situations.

My first unusual bird event happened when I was in my early twenties. As my then husband, Gordon, started to turn our old Pinto into the parking lot at the Dairy Queen, I noticed a large crow sitting about fifty feet off the ground on top of a steeple on the church beside the parking lot. For some reason, he held my attention. And as Gordon moved slowly forward, I watched in disbelief as the huge crow literally fell off the steeple and plummeted to the ground, landing directly in front of our car. Gordon hit the brakes and I jumped out of the car.

"Don't touch it!" Gordon yelled, as I bent down and picked it up.

There was a five-foot wide strip of grass at the back of the lot. I carried the bird over to the grass and lay it down, petting and stroking it while I pleaded with God to "please, please, please" let the large bird "wake up". After about a minute, the bird opened its eyes, rose to its feet, and flew off.

I know what you're thinking. Just another crow vs. car insurance scam. If it weren't for the fact that he never asked for our particulars, I would be inclined to agree.

Years later, I was working in a building located at a busy intersection of the downtown core, and decided to take a break and stroll by the shops on a narrow side street. It was a cool autumn afternoon and as I looked up at the bright blue sky I saw a pair of mallards flying high up in the distance. I paused to watch them. And as they flew overhead, they suddenly altered their flight path, mid-air. They were now descending and headed straight towards me.

I wondered to myself where and why they would land in a busy, noisy downtown area filled with skyscrapers. There was no water anywhere in the vicinity. As they kept descending I couldn't take my eyes off of them until, in unison, they glided to a perfect landing only fifteen feet in front of me. Our eyes locked. The mallards walked directly towards me and stopped. And stared.

I looked around to see if there was some possible reason for them to land at my feet, but could find nothing. It was just the mallards and me. We stood motionless, looking into each others' eyes. Then, I remembered the birdseed that I always carried in my pocket in the autumn (you heard right). So I took a little out and sprayed it onto the ground in front of me. They pecked around for a minute and then, as suddenly as they had arrived, flew away.

To this day I have trouble understanding what happened.

Fast-forward another several years, and I am walking our dog at the local dog park. It is a huge, forested area with a large open field in the center. It is close to dusk and I am just starting my walk. I let our one hundred and twenty-pound wolf-malamute hybrid, Miloup, off her leash and look up at the birds flying overhead. There are several individual birds and a small flock all headed in the same direction. As I am staring into the sky, one bird that was flying alone just stops, mid-flight, and drops down onto the ground directly in front of me. I don't mean "flies" down to the ground; I mean stops flapping its wings and drops out of the sky. It was at least a ten-story fall.

With so many loose dogs around, I was concerned for the welfare of the bird so I ran over and picked it up. It was a tiny Downy Woodpecker, and it didn't appear to be conscious. I hooked Miloup up to her leash and took the bird back to my car and put it on the seat to keep it safe while I took the dog for her walk.

When I got back to the car, the bird was still not moving, so I drove twenty minutes to the local bird sanctuary which was, by now, closed for the day. Fortunately there was a little box where you could place injured birds for safekeeping until the staff re-opened the next day.

The following morning I called to see if the little guy had survived. When Bob, the person who answered the phone, realized which bird I was talking about, he blurted out, "How did you catch him?"

"Catch him?" I said, "He fell out of the sky in front of me."

Bob was stunned. He told me he had never heard of such a thing, and said, "He was absolutely fine. He just flew away when we opened the box this morning."

Is it possible that the Downy Woodpecker had simply decided, mid-flight, that he needed a nap? We'll never know.

I didn't bother mentioning the black crow story to Bob. No point in having him wonder whether or not he should track me down as a possible threat to area wildlife.

Although it's just a guess, I'd bet money that somewhere in my one-sixteenth Native American background there was a relative named "falling bird".

Finally, perhaps the most unusual story of all occurred just last year. I was sitting on the front verandah on a very sunny afternoon when I noticed a large shadow move over the front lawn and heard a strange screeching sound I had never heard before. I knew a very large bird had to be soaring above our property, so I stepped off the verandah and looked up at the sky. Sure enough, a huge female red-tailed hawk was gliding in large circles above me. It was a thrilling sight, and I watched her intently as she slowly moved in circles until she passed over the distant horizon. Disappointed to see her go, I continued to stand there, wishing for her to come back so I could see her one more time.

No sooner had that thought crossed my mind than I saw her reappear on the horizon. She flew in the same broad, circular pattern, moving slowly back in my direction. Unbelievable though it may seem, and very much to my amazement, she not only returned to our property, she landed, directly facing me, on a low branch of a large oak tree only twenty feet from where I was standing. She sat perfectly still, staring at me. I felt like I could almost reach out and touch this most awesome creature. The rest of the world faded away as the human-hawk communion enveloped us. I didn't want to move. Couldn't move. Finally, I decided to chance stepping away to retrieve my camera. When I returned, she was gone. But it was impossible to be upset. She had given me one of the greatest gifts of my life.

I've never owned a pair of binoculars. I've never been a bird-watcher. But I do sometimes wonder if birds have been watching me.

Time for bed.

Goodnight, Dear Diary. Sleep tight, Mr. Boogie.

70. ONE RINGY-DINGY

Monday, October 3

Dear Diary:

It's taken me a while to get the hang of it, but one of the really great things about retirement is that you actually do have the time to discuss your service provider.
 So that is what I do. Not only do I speak with telemarketers that call, sometimes I call them. Have a telephone survey you want answered? I'm your gal.
 In fact, in the past ten months I have changed our cable and telephone service providers twice.
 If you call my number and ask for "the owner of the house", "the lady of the house" or even "John Smith", I will talk to you. Moreover, I will have questions for you. I will engage you to such a degree that you may have to call your supervisor for backup.
 So beware, once I have you on the hook, you will earn any money you make. Side effects of catching me at home? Anxiety, stomach upset, headache, nausea, possible numbness in the hands and feet. By the time I am finished, you will be pining for those people who just hang up on you. You may ultimately feel the need to put me on a "do not call" list. Pretty sure that's happened.
 Another benefit to being retired? There is also no limit to the amount of time I am prepared to take or effort I am prepared to expend to make sure that the dollar and thirty-seven cents you overcharged me on my utility bill is credited back to me. I believe that utility companies consider overcharges to be acceptable because the likelihood of any employed (read "sane") person wasting an hour and a half of their time to recover a few cents is pretty low. In terms of risk management, they have probably concluded that the risk of being caught padding a bill is worth the additional revenue from the thousands of customers who either won't notice or will give up in frustration trying to get the credit.
 I am a utility company's worst nightmare. I have no problem with taking five minutes to enter all the numerical information required to get past the automated customer service menu and on to the *musak* portion of my contact with your business. I will then

happily stay on the line as long as it takes to have a human customer service representative speak to me in person, despite the fact that you have warned me that, "The wait time is estimated to be thirty minutes." If your call center employee "inadvertently" cuts me off (like that's never on purpose), I will call back. Not only will I call back, I will send emails and letters by post to your company registering a complaint about "operator 612" or "Jason" and provide precise details of the date and time I called so that even if you misidentified your operator number or name to me they will be able to track you down.

Their dealings with me will eat into so much of their profit that they will never overcharge me again. At least six of their employees will be required to intervene, using a minimum of four man-hours (sixty-four dollars) to "resolve" the issue. They will inevitably give me my credit (one dollar and thirty-seven cents) plus "a little something for my trouble" (ten dollars). That dollar thirty-seven they tried to steal from me will cost them a total of somewhere in the neighborhood of seventy-five dollars and thirty-seven cents. Actually, seventy-four dollars. The dollar thirty-seven was never theirs in the first place. Retirement power!

And if you think nobody's paying any attention to that article on page six of the newspaper about one little public transportation proposed route change, think again. We, the retired, will be all over that situation. Well, to be fair, retired people and stay-at-home moms. Because we are the only people who take (read "have") the time to read the entire newspaper, make notes, think about it, do some research and craft letters to the editor on the subject. In fact, if they insisted that people who submit letters to the editor tick off whether they are a) retired b) a stay-at-home mom, or c) "other", almost nobody would tick off "other".

...Ooo...there's a 1(800) number calling in. Got to go.

Goodnight, Dear Diary.

71. JEDI MIND TRICKERY

Friday, October 7

Dear Diary:

Lucy is an amazing dog. So amazing, in fact, that sometimes we feel like the trailer park parents of a child prodigy; like just maybe we're "holding her back". Can she ever "be all that she can be" with us as parents?

We never really needed to train her to do anything. She is completely self-taught, always watching us and deciding for herself which tasks are most suited to her abilities. In fact, I'm pretty sure when she looks at the way I do things sometimes, she's thinking, "…amateur."

She's actually too smart for her own good. When I used to give her the hand signal to "sit", she would immediately "rollover" because she knew the order in which the commands were going to come was always "sit", "down" then "rollover". "Yeah. Yeah. Let's cut to the chase." So she has effectively trained me to mix up the order of the commands if I really want to see her do all three.

The day she turned four months old I wondered if, with the right training, maybe she could retrieve the newspaper from the end of our hundred-foot-long driveway. I was getting tired of doing my Tony Soprano act every morning, shuffling down the driveway in my white terry bathrobe and slippers. And those were the good days. We get freezing rain up here. And snow, lots of snow. I thought it would be fantastic if Lucy could eventually learn to fetch the paper. So, with a certain hopefulness, I opened the door that morning and let Lucy accompany me to pick up the newspaper. As I picked it up, I said the word, "newspaper". The next morning, as I was opening the door I said, "So, should we go and get the newspaper?" with every expectation that she would follow me and I would repeat yesterday's lesson. But before the door was even completely open, Lucy was sitting in front of me with the newspaper in her mouth. I thought to myself, "Wow. You are one awesome dog!" Pretty sure Lucy was thinking, "Next?"

When Martin is either too busy or away, Lucy "lets" me play catch with her, but insists that I do it her way, with two balls. If I

157

only bring one ball to play with, she finds the second ball and drops it at my feet. Only then can we start playing catch. "Mom! How many times do I have to explain this to you?" Apparently, the balls have to be lobbed with very precise timing so that there is no more than a half a second between her bringing the first one back and me throwing the second. "Chop. Chop. Let's keep this game moving!"

When you acquire a German Shepherd Dog you have to understand that your safety will be their Prime Directive - for life. Lucy has never needed a leash. Leashes are for family dogs that go out "for a walk". When Lucy accompanies us on our walk, she is actually "on patrol", establishing a security perimeter around us appropriate to the prevailing "Threat Level". We call it "the circle of love". A squirrel, cat or high wind is a Threat Level One; an unfamiliar noise, a Threat Level Two; familiar canines or humans are Threat Level Three; unfamiliar human females rate a Threat Level Four, and unfamiliar canines accompanied by familiar humans warrant a Threat Level Five. She saves her most audacious guarding and protecting behavior for unfamiliar, unaccompanied canines (Threat Level Seven), unfamiliar human males (Threat Level Nine) and anything travelling at unacceptable speed in our direction. If you are in an ATV headed towards us she will take you out. You and your ATV. You are a Threat Level Ten.

Needless to say, we have no need for a doorbell or an alarm system. And if you have work to do in our house, you will not be doing it "unaccompanied".

Lucy also "talks". And when we return to the house after any period of time we receive a full report of all goings on during our absence, delivered with as many nuances in inflection, tone and volume as any human being could muster. Although these reports are not always easy to interpret precisely, I think I've at least finally figured out what she's saying when she gives me a high-pitched double bark as I'm filling her food dish. I'm almost positive it's, "Supersize me!"

Perhaps the most impressive of her many talents though, is that she appears to have mastered the Jedi Mind Trick. We all know that the Force can have a powerful effect on the weak-minded, a phenomenon Jedi sometimes take advantage of in pursuing their missions. An experienced Jedi can use the Force to implant a suggestion in your mind, encouraging you to comply with the Jedi's wishes. There can be no other explanation for why I find myself doing her bidding for no apparent reason. I can be working diligently at my computer one minute, and the next thing I know my hand is reaching into Lucy's treat jar.

The only real concern I have at all about Lucy is that, lately, I think I've noticed a subtle, fleeting, lack of terror in her eyes whenever she encounters Twink. I'm not exactly sure when it began, and I'm not entirely comfortable with it. I believe she is starting to suspect that she could "take" the cat - if she really wanted to. Must keep an eye on that.

Then, of course, there's the age-old question about what we will do when "something happens" to Lucy. Everybody goes through the same thing when a beloved pet dies. They say that people often grieve more for their furry companions than for their spouses. And there's a reason for that. Your pet never judges you, never says or does anything mean or out of passive-aggressive spite, never cares if you're having a "bad hair" day or, overnight, a giant zit has appeared between your eyes. They are loyal. They love you (or in Lucy's case, "protect" you) unconditionally.

When a pet dies it feels like your heart has actually broken, and it can take a long time before you are able to open yourself up again to that kind of love. Hopefully Lucy will live a long and healthy life. We discovered recently that she has EPI (exocrine pancreatic insufficiency) after watching her lose twenty percent of her body weight in a matter of weeks. It's under control now with enzymes, so we'll keep our fingers crossed that she has another dozen years left if we're lucky. We will be seventy-two years old. At that point, we will have to think twice before running out and buying a pet that has every possibility of outliving us. A kitten, for example, could go on for another twenty years. I'm not all that confident we'll be around for the twenty years it could take to see that kitten through to the end of its natural life. We will have to at least weigh the likelihood of us croaking before the cat does. How's my heart? My blood pressure? Do I have diabetes? And at seventy-two you certainly don't want to go falling in love with a pet like a baby parrot. Macaws can live for eighty years. Before considering any new pet when you are seventy-two years old you will have to ask yourself some tough questions and think about your general physical condition. Will you be able to lob a ball in five years? Ten years? Sure you can get a little dog that doesn't require long walks and won't drag you bodily down the street like an Iditarod sled run amok, but Chihuahuas live a long time. Will you?

I think when we have to say goodbye to Lucy, maybe that will be the end of it for us, unless maybe I find an older dog that needs to be adopted staring up at me from the classified section of the newspaper. It's a miracle we don't already have seven or seventeen dogs. Well, maybe not so much a miracle as living in compliance with local bylaws.

Think I'll go stick the "Pet of the Month" sticker on Lucy's portrait in the hall. Mr. Boogie has already won four times in a row, and Twink doesn't appear to really care what anyone thinks of her.

Goodnight, Dear Diary.

72. SEVENTY-TWO HOURS

Tuesday, October 11

Dear Diary:

There was a time when Martin would make a joke about it if he caught me wearing the same tank top during the day that I had slept in the night before.

Apparently, now I have up to four days before he actually notices that I've been wearing the same clothes 24/7. Although, to be perfectly candid, I'm not one hundred percent certain he would have noticed even then if I had bothered to shower at some point during that ninety-six hours. So, by my calculations, if I either change clothes or shower every seventy-two hours, I can avoid another embarrassing confrontation about my "personal hygiene". Probably best to keep that under control.

But it's not like I'm "unhygienic". I do put clean underwear on every day. And just this afternoon, Sarah and I had quite a lengthy discussion about hygiene products.

Neither of us could understand why anyone ever buys anything other than Charmin Ultra Soft toilet paper. You can really learn a lot about people just by using their powder rooms when you visit. And who uses bars of soap anymore? Gross! But don't put out antibacterial soap unless you want to burn the skin off of everyone's hands. Also, if I had my way, we'd have a paper towel dispenser in the powder room. Nobody wants to "dry" their hands on a damp towel the size of a large facecloth that's been sitting in your powder room for a week. Yuck. And when it comes to paper towels, we were in complete agreement that there is no explanation for buying any other brand than Bounty select-a-size. Why would you? Does anybody? Our one minor point of disagreement was on facial tissue, but that probably had more to do with money than anything else. Sarah can afford the "name brand" tissues that are three-ply with lotion. Sure, if money is no object those are great, but for a lot less money I get Kirkland's facial tissues and they're pretty good. ...Oh my god what is wrong with me? Why am I talking about toilet paper?

I shouldn't get so defensive about one little snide remark.

Stupid Martin. Maybe I'll show him his nose hair in my 20X magnification mirror. Then let's see if he brings up my "hygiene" again.

    Yeah. That's mature. Goodnight, Dear Diary.

73. MORE SCHMANCY THAN FANCY

Saturday, October 15

Dear Diary:

Today I started dabbling with the whole concept of using recipes for cooking.

Usually I tend to cook versions of the same meals over and over again. If I have lean ground beef, I make spaghetti sauce. I always have diced tomatoes and tomato sauce in the cupboard, Parmesan cheese and baguettes in the freezer. The leftover sauce gets used for a pasta casserole topped with shredded cheeses. We also always have a couple of roasts, bags of split chicken wings and pork chops in the freezer. Typically, I just add cooked rice or potatoes and some coleslaw, carrots, broccoli, green beans, peas or corn. Pretty basic stuff. In a desperate moment I might resort to an omelet. If I'm feeling inspired, I'll add a pepper jelly glaze to the meat or stir-fry sliced chicken breasts and vegetables in ginger and garlic or sweet and sour sauce. I'll make the occasional beef and barley soup in the winter, and throw together a lot of basic salads with romaine, celery, cucumber, red peppers and hard-boiled eggs in the summer. I might even toss a turnip into my winter stew every once in a while. But I've generally tried to avoid pouring over recipes and making special trips to the store for miniscule amounts of special ingredients that I'll probably never use again.

You might say that I learned the hard way to just stick to what I know works. Although by the time Martin and I met I had conquered food basics, I still remember the first time I ever made spaghetti sauce for my ex-husband. We were having company over for dinner and I decided I would make my own spaghetti sauce from scratch. How was I supposed to know that "allspice" didn't live up to its name?

Of course I can't be certain that my lack of cooking skills was actually the reason my first marriage ended in divorce, but if I were to hazard a guess, I would say that it's not beyond the realm of possibilities that it was a contributing factor. Gordon never got tired of telling everybody about the time I tried to bake him a birthday cake from a mix. I know. Foolproof, right? Wrong.

I thought I was being pretty fancy when I picked out a cherry flavored cake mix. You have to understand that I came from a home where my mother never baked cakes. It was always pies, homemade pies of every description. I used to envy my friends whose mothers baked cakes. Anyway, all excuses aside, I was in our new apartment with my new husband, and I wanted to bake him a birthday cake. It was going to be a cherry layer cake with butter cream frosting and slivered maraschino cherries on top.

I followed the directions carefully (add water and one egg), put the pans in the oven and waited. When the buzzer sounded I took them out of the oven and set them on cooling racks. They were pale pink and smelled and looked amazing. When I looked at them an hour later, I couldn't believe my eyes. Both cakes appeared to be sunken and unusually moist. I touched my finger to the center of one and the entire "cake" collapsed into what could only be described as a pink swamp. Luckily, Gordon hadn't arrived home yet, so I attempted a rescue operation.

The trouble was, while what was in the middle was lumpy and squishy, certain areas around the edges and tops already appeared to be crusty. What to do? My thinking was that if for some reason the cakes weren't cooked enough, then more cooking would fix everything. But it didn't seem to me that sticking them back in the oven "as is" was the way to go. My solution was to scrape everything out of the pans into my large mixing bowl and try to "mix" what could only be described as a giant bowl of pink sludge "back into" a batter. So there I stood for ten minutes, hand-beaters whirring away at the chunks of cooked cherry cake and pink goo, trying desperately to re-liquefy the whole thing.

Clearly, chemistry had never been my forte. For those of you who might be equally challenged, I can confirm that you cannot re-liquefy pieces of cake into a batter simply by trying to beat them into submission. Even when you have added a significant amount of sludge-like material into the mix.

Undaunted, I turned the oven back on, dumped the "mixture" back into the cake pans, mashed it all down as evenly as possible, and put them back in the oven.

What came out of the oven a half-hour later could not have been described as "cake". In fact, what came out of the oven a half-hour later literally defied description. And that is the precise moment when Gordon arrived home. Did I ruin his birthday? Probably, but not on purpose - despite what he claimed.

Fortunately, Martin has never been witness to … well, if I'm going to be completely honest … let me leave it at admitting that I haven't been "allowed" to use the BBQ ever since the chicken breast disaster of 1989. Or, as Martin still calls it, "Firestorm Friday".

But tomorrow night? Tomorrow night we will be dining on curried scallops, chicken Alsacienne, buttered noodles and green beans with pine nuts, and raspberry parfaits for dessert. I assume it'll be okay to use milk instead of heavy cream. And I have some liverwurst in the fridge - which is almost the same thing as pate de foie, right? Also, I can't see how it could be a problem if I use up my walnuts instead of going out to get pine nuts. What are pine nuts, anyway? And hopefully I don't actually "need" arrowroot. How important can one little teaspoon of something really be?

Goodnight, Dear Diary. Wish me luck!

74. HOCUS BOGUS

Thursday, October 20

Dear Diary:

Martin and I had a little "talk" today after he had conducted some sort of a review of our budget. Apparently, I have the power to make money "disappear".

That got me thinking. And, although it would seem that I don't actually need lessons, I spent a good part of the afternoon researching how I might be able to become a real magician.

Fascinating stuff. And they almost had me hooked. In fact, I was ready to sign up for online classes until I read some pretty specific advice, "You will be poor for many years."

Realizing that would never do, I moved on to looking up cute baby animals on YouTube. Two hours later I was reviewing my browsing history to get back to a really funny animal video when I noticed something. I hadn't actually looked up "how to become a magician". I had looked up "how to become a musician". Stupid auto correct.

Fortunately, the mood had passed. And in truth, capes have never been my thing.

Got to vanish. Goodnight, Dear Diary.

75. WOULD YOU LIKE FRIES WITH THAT?

Wednesday, October 26

Dear Diary:

I have taken to resenting people with jobs. Sometimes I even resent people in movies and on TV who have jobs.

Everywhere I turn people have jobs. They always seem to be laughing and enjoying themselves, or having interesting little "job" dramas. Some of them have uniforms. They all have "schedules". They get paychecks. They get to say things like, "I'm so exhausted," and "I have to work late." They get to have lunch breaks, and go to office parties. They set their alarm clocks every night and get to rush around in the morning to get ready for "work". They grab a quick shower, put on nice clothes and get to fix their hair and make-up. They get to go to meetings with other adults, probably with coffee and muffins too. They get to "chat" with their colleagues about all the gossip in the office and rush around on their lunch hours to the bank or to pick something up at the pharmacy. They think they're so smart just because they have "jobs".

Today was a real low. As I was sitting at the pickup window at McDonald's staring blankly at the teenager with the headset on, a thought crossed my mind…I could do that.

Maybe I'll set my alarm tonight. I just want to have that feeling again. Like there's somewhere that I "have" to be that doesn't involve a medical professional or my mother; or worse, a medical professional and my mother.

Maybe if I join a gym. Take yoga? I have got to pull myself together.

Goodnight, Dear Diary. Thank God I have you.

76. TRICKY TREAT

Monday, October 31

Dear Diary:

Today was Halloween.
 I love Halloween, probably because it's a harbinger to Thanksgiving and Christmas. When the kids were here we always did Halloween up big. Not big as in, "I warned you not to go to the Olsen house - those people are crazy" big, but with lots of carved pumpkins, dangling skeletons, cobwebs, spooky lighting and a fog machine. I always wore a witch's hat and blacked out a front tooth, and Martin put on a scary rubber facemask and yelled "Boo!" from the sidelines. Pretty tame stuff, really, but we got a kick out of it. We never carved our pumpkins or put our decorations out until the "day of". Instead, Martin and I got everything setup so that when the kids got home from school we would have the Olsen family Halloween version of the *Shmenge Brothers' Christmas* that we called the "carving of the pumpkins ceremony", which also included letting the kids put all the finishing touches on the outdoor décor. Finally, before the kids got their costumes on, we all stuffed little bags with various types of Halloween candy and tied them closed with black and orange ribbons.
 But "big" Halloweens are now a part of our past. It's been years since we've put out anything other than one or two pumpkins on the front verandah. We started to feel a little creepy about dressing up the house for all the neighborhood kids when ours were grown and gone. Sort of like the house with the weird old childless couple who are trying just a little bit too hard to lure children to their front door. And this year we even nixed the little individually filled, beribboned bags and opted for the Costco boxes of full-sized (peanut free) chocolate bars.
 Perhaps not so surprisingly, the Trick-or-Treaters appeared to be more than happy to have a full-sized chocolate bar instead of a bunch of mini candies. I guess it was just we parents who thought the little mini treats were "cuter". Kids aren't stupid. Even the five-year-olds could see this was a way better deal. I heard one of them excitedly telling his friends as they were coming up the driveway and he was

leaving, "They've got real chocolate bars!"

It's probably just as well that my trip to the craft store in the mall failed so miserably. I'm not sure homemade cupcakes hand decorated with orange icing and tiny witches, pumpkins and goblins would have gone over all that well. To say nothing of the fact that "Have a cupcake," almost begs to be followed by the phrase, "My little pretties."

I still remember when I was a kid actually getting homemade popcorn balls at Halloween. Of course that was before all the weirdoes started putting razor blades into apples and lacing homemade items with drugs. Some treats are tricky.

As for those full-sized chocolate bars? Looks like our calculations paid off. We have just enough "leftovers" to indulge our chocolate addictions for the next week. It's not quite as much fun as it was raiding the kids' goody bags when they were asleep, but at least we can drown our nostalgia in chocolate.

Happy Halloween, Dear Diary. Goodnight.

77. THINGS THAT MAKE YOU GO "AAH"

Thursday, November 3

Dear Diary:

Whenever I was upset as a child, my Dad always used to make me write out a list of ten things that made me feel good. And of course, by the time I had finished focusing on all the things that made me feel good, I didn't feel bad any longer. Smart Dad. I guess it was his version of "count your blessings". Never a bad idea.

Anyway, I was feeling pretty down this morning, so I resurrected my Dad's old trick and tried to come up with a list of things that make me smile. The trouble is, when you're a grownup, with adult worries and struggles, it's not quite as easy to do as when your biggest worry is "Sandra likes Maureen better than me," or "My clothes are stupid." In fact, trying to think of anything (besides alcohol) that might make me feel better was a difficult exercise. But I finally conquered my mood with this list. And, as you can see, once I got going I almost couldn't stop:

1. A cup of hot tea with a Mallomar cookie. Aah
2. Napping on the verandah. Aah
3. Watching puppies. Aah
4. The smell of a turkey roasting in the oven. Aah
5. The first after-dinner sip of Bailey's in coffee. Aah
6. A plate of homemade crepes, pure maple syrup and crisp bacon on a Sunday morning. Aah
7. Clean sheets. Aah
8. Curling up under our down duvet on a chilly night. Aah
9. The sound of the Canada Geese arriving in the spring. Aah
10. The sound of the Canada Geese leaving in the autumn. (Draw your own conclusions.) Aah
11. Hummingbirds. Aah
12. First snowfall. Aah
13. Sitting in front of a crackling fire (in a fireplace). Aah
14. Seeing the sun filtering through the bright pink leaves of our maple tree in autumn. Aah
15. The first day in spring when I get to wear sandals again. Aah

16. Standing on the front lawn when Martin turns on the outdoor Christmas lights. Aah

17. Every time Martin yells downstairs, "The internet is back on!" Double Aah

Life is a pretty awesome gift. It probably doesn't hurt to remind myself of that every now and again.

Sweet dreams to me. Goodnight, Dear Diary.

78. DESERT ISLAND GAME

Monday, November 7

Dear Diary:

I actually forgot to set the clocks back an hour yesterday. Like that ever happened when I was working. Like it matters now that I'm not. As long as I don't have an appointment, it's kind of nice to have the day revolve around me, rather than have me revolve around what the correct time is. Sweet.

Anyway, I've been thinking that you can learn a lot about people by asking them what books they would take with them if they were going to be stranded on a desert island for the rest of their lives. And I spent some time this afternoon seriously considering the question myself - you know, in case I accidentally fall into a wormhole in the space-time continuum that takes me back to high school.

But I actually had fun figuring out what books I would want to read or refer to over and over again in my life as a castaway. Most of it, as it turns out, wouldn't qualify as "great literature". I'd let someone else on the island bring *War and Peace*. But I bet more people would be fetching me coconuts and offering to spear a fish for my dinner for a chance to borrow one of my books:

1. The Harry Hole Series (All ten books from *The Bat* to *Police*) (Jo Nesbo) - for when the thrill of being stranded on a desert island is gone. And at least I'll get to read about snow even if I never see it again.

2. *Skeleton Crew* (Stephen King) - for when the animals, reptiles and insects on the island and the fear of never seeing home again don't scare you quite enough.

3. *The Unexpurgated Code - a complete manual of survival & manners* (J.P. Donleavy) - upon being stranded on a desert isle one must never give in to the baser human instincts. To say nothing of the fact that maintaining a sense of humor on the island will be critical.

4. *A Brief History of Time* (Stephen W. Hawking) - for perspective.

5. *The Fabric of the Cosmos* (Brian Greene) - for understanding perspective.

6. *The Deptford Trilogy (Fifth Business, The Manticore, World Of*

Wonders) (Robertson Davies) - the only nod to "great literature" in my list. The perfect antidote to the mystery, myth and magic of being stranded on a desert island, is an alternate story of mystery, myth and magic.

7. *The Holy Bible* (Douay-Rheims version or King James) - unsurpassed in its ability to stir up debate when the island gets boring - and people will want to have ceremonies (weddings, births, funerals).

8. *Waiting for the Barbarians* (J. M. Coetzee) - the title speaks for itself.

9. *Oxford English Dictionary* (Oxford University Press) - no need to stop using correct English just because we're stranded on an island.

10. *Transforming the Mind* (His Holiness the Dalai Lama) - for learning acceptance.

I didn't choose any medical texts because - well, with no access to medical testing or prescription medication, there's probably no point in sitting around guessing what disease you have contracted. Of course I would bring along the basic medicine cabinet contents, Chewable Pepto Bismol, Tums Smoothies, Aspirin and Gas-X (all in "extra-strength" formulae).

I never understood why anybody ever buys "regular strength" of anything. If you have a headache, upset stomach, indigestion or bad gas, what on earth would make you choose a medication that is, by definition, less effective? Seriously?

Well, that's enough fantasy for one day. Think I'll go watch Netflix.

Goodnight, Dear Diary.

79. SURE, BUT CAN YOU DANCE?

Saturday, November 12

Dear Diary:

There were times when I thought I wasn't going to make it, but I am now officially a Grand Master at every one of the seventy-five levels of Peggle.

I was considering announcing my success to Martin, but for now I think I'll just keep this bit of information under my hat. Let it slip out at an appropriate time. Like it's no big deal.

Oh. I forgot to mention. For the past year, Martin has been playing Peggle whenever he takes a break from his programming. I downloaded it five days ago.

Only one problem. Not quite sure how to fill the void that is now my life. Make it two problems. Not sure my prescription lenses work any more.

I have to go close my eyes. Goodnight, Dear Diary.

80. HOME, HOME WITHOUT A RANGE

Wednesday, November 16

Dear Diary:

Well, my vision finally "came back" over the last couple of days, but my brain is still playing Peggle whenever I close my eyes. Hopefully that will go away soon. On the bright side, at least I've been able to read the newspaper again.

It's strange, but it seems like there are a lot more advertisements in the paper for "seniors residences" these days. Either that, or I've just started paying more attention to them. Maybe a little too much attention. Today, I actually ran across an ad that made me want to put the house up for sale. A two-bedroom unit with a kitchenette at Governor's Court sounded pretty darn appealing; gorgeous view of the river, beauty shop, ice-cream shop, whirlpool, café-bistro, housekeeping, a diverse calendar of activities and a highly respected executive chef.

I found myself fantasizing about all the freedom a new kind of "independent living" lifestyle could give us. No yard maintenance for Martin. No more trying to keep this four-bedroom house clean. No grocery shopping. No cooking. No dishes to do. People serving food to me. Every meal. Every day.

"Could I have bacon on the side with that, please?"

"Not a problem, Mrs. Olsen. Will there be anything else?"

No more arguing with Martin about whether or not it is morally acceptable to kill a mouse and her babies that he finds living in a drawer in the garage.

Not only did Governor's Court sound completely awesome, I was struggling to come up with even one reason why we would want to live anywhere else. I thought about my Dad's mother who, at ninety-five refused to even visit her friend in a retirement home.

"Why don't you want to spend a few hours with Sally, Gran?"

"I don't want to go to that place."

"Why not?"

"It's full of old people!"

There was no point in explaining to her that virtually every other person in "that place" was actually her junior. Which raised yet another point in favor of living at Governor's Court. At our ages, Martin and I would be like the new "hotties" on the block. Talk about make you feel young again.

In fact, I was pretty much emotionally committed to signing up, when Martin walked into the kitchen.

"What's that you're looking at?"

"It's this really cool retirement residence called Governor's Court."

"Isn't that where Sophie's Mom lives?"

And that was that. With the precision of a laser guided missile, Martin's simple question had obliterated the fantasy and brought me crashing back down to reality.

Yes, it would be weird to have Sophie and Dave drop by our "suite" to see us when they visit her Mom, to say nothing of the idea of moving into a seniors' residence before my eighty-three-year-old Mother does. And it's probably also true that my having even "less to do" wouldn't really be the answer to anything.

Well, I suppose I should go start the dishwasher before bed. Nobody else is going to do it.

Goodnight, Dear Diary.

81. AAARGH! *&%$#

Sunday, November 20

Dear Diary

Sunday night is "garbage night".

    It's the night when, before going to bed, I empty all the wastebaskets in the house, search for any half-eaten, out-of-date containers of yoghurt, sour cream or cottage cheese in the fridge, toss all the moldy items and "leftovers" that have lost their charm over the past week, and forage in the freezer for the bits of meat trimmings and congealed oil that have been stored for weekly disposal. I take the last kitchen compost bag out to the green bin at the side of the verandah, and put everything else in a large garbage bag, open the inside door to the garage, and blindly toss the bag in. I don't even turn on the light to see where it might land.

    And that is the precise moment when, every week, I am reminded about the state of the garage. It is always a sore point. Every Sunday night I trundle up to bed reminding myself of the fact that yet another week has gone by during which I have been unable to park my car in our garage like a normal person. I may be the only person on earth who, even when I was working, looked forward to Monday morning, because Sunday night was over for another week.

    Is it wrong to pray that I die before Martin does just so that I don't ever have to deal with all the crap in the garage?

    …On the other hand, there's always 1(800) GOTJUNK … and I'm pretty sure that the Cash For Trash telephone number is still on the bulletin board in the kitchen. Hmm. Perhaps I was being hasty.

    Goodnight, Dear Diary.

82. BAD JUJU

Friday, November 25

Dear Diary:

If I weren't just a little concerned that it might bring bad juju down on us, I would actually fall to my knees and thank God that Thanksgiving is over.

At least it was Sarah's turn to have Mom. Martin and I waved goodbye to Aksel and Camilla this afternoon, and all I did the rest of the day was watch Netflix and reheat some dinner left over from last night.

This year the kids are both coming for Christmas, so I sort of took advantage of the fact that it was just Martin, his folks and me for Thanksgiving dinner. Instead of getting up at 6:30 in the morning and spending all day preparing a twenty-five-pound roasted turkey with homemade gravy and stuffing, my secret cranberry sauce recipe and pumpkin pies made from scratch, I threw a "cook from frozen" turkey breast into the oven, tossed a box of dried stuffing mix into some boiling water, and opened a couple of cans of gravy and cranberry sauce. Dessert? A store-bought pumpkin pie with a can of spray whipped cream. I know. That alone could warrant some bad juju.

But while everyone else was naming all the things they were most thankful for before dinner, I was saying a personal "Thank you," ...to Butterball, Franco American, Ocean Spray, Costco and Reddi-Whip.

I think my homemade mashed potatoes and candied carrots may have confused them, because nobody uttered a word of complaint about the dinner. ...Hmm. Food for thought.

Goodnight, Dear Diary.

83. NOMENCLATURE

Tuesday, November 29

Dear Diary:

One of Martin's business associates had a pre-Christmas get-together this evening.
 Blah blah blah, blah blah blah. I simply don't like going to things where I don't know anyone and all the conversations are superficial and boring. No matter how they bill themselves, they aren't real parties. Nobody at a real party walks around with a smile permanently plastered on their face. It's unnatural. And when you hear laughter at a real party, it's real laughter - because somebody has actually said something funny. Not the "I should pretend to be mildly amused" fake laughter that people use when they don't really know you and what you are saying isn't really all that funny.
 On top of my general displeasure with having had to shower and dress up to attend the event, after only about a half an hour of meeting new people I got fed up with answering the "And what do you do?" question by saying "I'm retired."
 It would appear that saying "I'm retired" at a business gathering is the social equivalent of saying, "I have herpes" at a singles dance. In addition to sounding disturbingly similar to "I'm retarded," it also seems to palpably suggest to the listener, "I have zero potential," and "I can offer you nothing and I will never need your services."
 So I did what any bored person does at a business gathering. I started making things up. I began slowly, first testing the waters with "I'm between jobs right now," but when that wasn't met with anything more than a "knowing" glance, I moved on.
 As it turned out, "I count calories," and "Right now I'm juicing," weren't quite the amusing responses that I had expected they might be, eliciting little more than quizzical looks and excuses for turning around and leaving. They had to know I was joking, right?
 Anyway, it wasn't too long before I finally struck gold when, on yet another whim, I tried out, "I was fired."
 This may come as a surprise, and I'm not exactly sure why it is the case, but saying "I was fired" at a business gathering, no matter how softly and quietly spoken, is the social equivalent of saying, "I

won the lottery" at a family reunion. From all corners of the room, people start moving towards you, until a crowd is encircling you, hanging on your every word. The adult equivalent of a good ghost story, "I was fired" seems to play on every working person's deepest, darkest fear. Presumably on the assumption that "forewarned is forearmed", without asking the question directly, what I think they are really searching for is insider information on "the five warning signs that you are about to be fired".

But the thirst for information doesn't stop there. What's the latest scoop on severance packages? The more information they demanded, the more I made up. How long had I worked there? I went with twelve years; long enough so they would know that they could never feel secure. What day of the week was it? I said, "Tuesday". Wow. That threw them for a loop. What time of day? 1:30 p.m. "Outrageous!" "They waited until after lunch?" "They made you gather your stuff up in front of everybody?" They were all imagining their own humiliation at the same time that they were reveling in mine. It's a statistics game. The more people they knew who were fired, the lower the probability that they would be next.

Just as I was really getting going - impending lawsuits, wrongful dismissal, likely time-frame for settlement - I noticed Martin hovering at the far edge of the crowd that had gathered. He caught my eye, and I knew the jig was up.

As we were trying to make a graceful exit a number of people came up to shake my hand. "Good luck with everything," they said sincerely. "Please. Keep us posted."

"What is wrong with you?" was all Martin said on the whole drive home.

Almost positive that "I was bored" would sound worse than saying nothing, I refused to answer on the grounds that I might have incriminated myself.

I'll apologize tomorrow. Maybe there is something wrong with me.

Goodnight, Dear Diary.

84. CHEERS!

Thursday, December 1

Dear Diary:

Today was the first day of December, one of my favorite days of the year.

December the first is the day we set up all our Christmas decorations and outdoor lights. For the next thirty-seven days our house will be so filled with the sights, the sounds and the smells of Christmas that anyone who enters could be forgiven for believing that our front door is actually a portal to 1962.

I can't get enough of Christmas. This is my time of year. Even retirement can't put a damper on Christmas.

The very first thing I did was take everything off the mantel above the fireplace and pack it away. Then I set about making the mantel sacred ground, the place where I set up our ceramic nativity scene. There are three wise men, a camel, a donkey, a shepherd boy, Saint Joseph, the Blessed Virgin Mary and the baby Jesus, who lies in the center of the mantel on a tiny fur blanket tucked into His crib. Then I placed small, silver tea-light holders with star-shaped holes in them beside each of the six-inch figurines, and hung a large silver star on the wall above the baby Jesus.

Next, I retrieved Rudolph from the top shelf in my office closet. When I first found Rudolph at a store, he was just an eight-inch-high by fourteen-inch-long painted plaster figure of a deer lying with his legs tucked under him and his head erect. He had the most beautiful, big, glassy brown eyes I had ever seen. Although I did notice that he had no antlers and was therefore probably meant to be a "she", in the spirit of Christmas, and with what is probably best characterized as a suspension of disbelief, I chose to think of him as a "he" and called him Rudolph. What would be the point of insisting on imbuing one tiny decorative element of Christmas with logic? I had great things in mind for that little deer. So, I brought him home and transformed him into Rudolph by painting his nose with high-gloss "Chinese Red" nail polish and putting a wreath of red and green jingle bells around his neck. Even though his nose doesn't actually blink, he certainly lights up the room and makes everybody smile. His place of honor is center stage on top of the dining room buffet, and almost everybody has made it clear that if I ever "get tired" of him, he will have a good home with them. Silly people. Rudolph isn't going anywhere.

Then out came the large, musical, ceramic rocking horse laden with Christmas packages, the sandbag Santa all dressed in white and the Saint Nicholas wearing a crown of mistletoe, cloaked in green velvet and carrying a green velvet bag overflowing with tiny gifts. Next come the Christmas village, the wooden sleigh stuffed with toys for the hearth, the glittery green garlands resplendent with gold, silver and red velvet poinsettia flowers for draping around the picture windows and the colored LED icicle lights to festoon the inside of the patio doors in the kitchen. And of course Christmas wouldn't really be Christmas without the red and green jingle bell wreath for the front door, the red and green wreath for the center of the living room picture window, the red felt bell-shaped jingle bell door hangers, the bowls of cinnamon and clove scented potpourri, gold-glittered pinecones, boughs of greenery and multitude of other Christmas paraphernalia distributed with abandon throughout the house. Even the bathrooms are now filled with special Christmas decorations and candles.

While I was seeing to all of that, Martin was outside checking and hanging all the multi-colored outdoor lights. He hasn't quite mastered the Chevy Chase million watt extravaganza, but he's getting there - minus any hitches.

By the time he was finished with the outdoor lights, I was ready for him to haul the eight-foot "I can't believe it's not real" Christmas tree up from the basement. With all the concern over fire hazards, we decided many years ago to not use a real tree. It may also have had something to do with the fact that real trees always attracted way too much interest from our pets, and it's hard to get a real tree to stay in great shape for thirty-seven days.

But before getting to the tree, Martin and I walked down to the street in front of our house and, remote control in hand, Martin counted to three and then switched on all the outdoor lights. Funny what a thrill that is, even at our age. After standing there staring at the lights for a few minutes as if we'd never seen such a beautiful sight before, we went inside, reconfigured the living room furniture, and Martin set the tree up in the corner next to the fireplace. I put on some Christmas music, made us a couple of rum and eggnogs as per our tradition, and we started the decorating.

What was once a wonderful family tradition is actually still just as special when it's only Martin and me doing the decorating. We paused over each ornament, recalling the year we had bought or received each one, or how little the kids were when they presented them to us as gifts. Great thought was given to where each bird, sparkly pinecone, tasseled star, jingle bell, Santa Claus, toque-wearing puppy, dangling Christmas cookie, candy cane, beaded satin ball and Disney character was placed. No corner was left bare. Since tinsel has never been an option with pets in the house, when the tree was almost done we added the finishing touch, the twisted, colored aluminum icicles, which provide just the right amount of glitter and shimmer. For the grand finale, I decided to add popcorn garlands this year, to give the tree a super-traditional, old-fashioned look and feel.

When everything on the tree was in place, I hung the stockings from the mantel (including Lucy's new "Good Dog" stocking with twelve jingle bells around the top), we sat down on the sofa with our drinks and Martin turned on the lights....things that make you go "aah".

It's Christmas time again, and all is well in the Olsen house. Cheers!

Goodnight, Dear Diary.

85. HOW MANY IS THAT?

Monday, December 5

Dear Diary:

It has taken me three days to start feeling even remotely sensible again after what I discovered when I came downstairs Saturday morning.
    Bad things are not supposed to interfere with Christmas. Christmas is my happy time.
    Tell that to Lucy, who apparently didn't approve of her "Good Dog" stocking. I woke up Saturday morning to discover that she had not only taken her stocking down off the mantel, she had removed every one of the twelve jingle bells from the cuff and they had disappeared. The stocking was made in China. I think it's a safe guess that the jingle bells were not made of anything as harmless as stainless steel. In fact, I suspected they could very well contain lead. When they were nowhere to be found in the house, we had no choice but to spend the next three days "searching" through all of Lucy's poops until we were satisfied that we had found all twelve jingle bells.
    "Got another one!"
    "How many is that?"
    And to make matters worse, "somebody" had pulled and chewed at all the popcorn garlands on our Christmas tree.
    While the "proof was in the poop" as far as the jingle bells were concerned, there was no clear evidence linking Lucy to the popcorn incident. And she certainly wasn't behaving as though she bore any responsibility for it. Also, I may have detected a whiff of stale popcorn on Twink's breath. But whoever was to blame, the whole tree was a mess, and had to be completely re-done. Trust me when I tell you, I was not "feeling the magic" the second time around.
    I wonder if they make a "Bad Dog" stocking.
    And then today I had to go and make the mistake of looking into my 20x magnification mirror. At first, I thought the mirror must have been distorting what I was seeing, so I went into the bathroom to check it out in the big mirror. There was no distortion. My left ear lobe is at least a half-inch longer than my right ear lobe. How is it that I never noticed this before? Did it happen overnight? I tried

"tucking" it under with tape. I even considered folding and stapling it. What if I just took scissors and lopped the excess skin off? Would it heal okay? I can't go around with one elongated earlobe "wobbling to and fro". Have people been talking about my ear lobe behind my back? Humming cruel ditties, "Can you tie them in a knot? Can you tie them in a bow?" to themselves every time they see me?

This is even worse than when I realized that what I had thought was just a "pillow crease" that appeared one morning beside my right eye six months ago is never going to go away. Lesson learned. Always sleep on your back when you're "past a certain age", or you don't know what kind of permanent damage you might do. But how am I supposed to deal with an ear deformity? I can never wear earrings again. It's that simple.

Well, there are thirty-two days of "Christmas Joy" left. What else could go wrong?

Goodnight, Dear Diary.

86. WILL THAT BE IN A CUP OR A BOWL?

Friday, December 9

Dear Diary:

I was sitting down at the kitchen table this morning enjoying a bowl of Lucky Charms when, for the second time in my life, I discovered new and startling information right there on the cereal box.

Apparently, a "serving" of Lucky Charms is only three quarters of a cup.

Why would they do that? Who eats three quarters of one cup of Lucky Charms? Why not identify the calories and nutrients in a normal sized bowl, which, by my calculation, would be more like one and a half or two cups? I defy anyone to take a one-cup measuring cup, fill it only three quarters full, add milk, and try to convince themselves that they have had a "serving" of cereal. I'm pretty sure you can't even dip anything more than one of those tiny coffee spoons into a one-cup measuring cup. What is that, a leprechaun serving?

Not only that, but they also have the audacity to inform you of the caloric and nutritional consequences of adding one half of a cup of "skim" milk. Is that supposed to be a joke? Does anyone ever add "skim" milk to Lucky Charms? My guess is that people (like me) who actually buy boxes of Lucky Charms are an entirely different species to people who buy skim milk. You won't ever see those two items in the same shopping cart at the grocery store. Go ahead. Canvas your local grocery store cashiers - they're going to tell you I'm right. The skim milk people are the ones whose carts are filled with kale, quinoa, plain yoghurt and tofu. We Lucky Charms people are the ones who pile our carts full of bacon, hot dogs, frozen waffles, Little Debbie snacks and Cheez Whiz. The fact that "cheese" is spelled "Cheez" should probably be a bit of a red flag, but the heart wants what the heart wants.

Do the manufacturers seriously suspect that people are selecting Lucky Charms as a diet food? Or that we are eating Lucky Charms for health reasons? I'm pretty sure that if you are having a bowl of Lucky Charms you are not counting every calorie you consume because, let's face it, if you are counting calories your choice will be either dinner tonight or this bowl of Lucky Charms. People are not idiots. They eat Lucky Charms for one reason and one reason only, they taste amazing!

And the only way to eat Lucky Charms is by filling your cereal bowl, adding enough whole or 2% milk so that there will be some left over, eating the bowl of cereal, pouring more Lucky Charms into the excess milk, and finishing that off as well. Nobody is taking three quarters of one cup of Lucky Charms, adding a half a cup of skim milk and eating that with a tiny coffee spoon and saying "Wow! That was magically delicious!"

I'm not saying that we should fill giant mixing bowls with Lucky Charms. But there is a big difference between a normal serving of any food and what manufacturers are claiming a "suggested" serving should be.

Have these people never been to Florida? In Florida, an average single serving is enough to feed a family of four. I'll never forget the time we went out to lunch with our friends Sandy and Leonard in Miami and Leonard ordered borscht. The waitress asked him, "Will that be in a cup or a bowl?" In hindsight, I suppose we should have understood that to be code for "Are you a human being or a hippopotamus?" because when his "bowl" of borscht arrived, it was in a family-sized salad bowl into the center of which they had dropped an entire pint of sour cream.

My guess is that a number of people in Florida are not paying attention to the "serving" guidelines on the side of the Lucky Charms box (or anywhere else, for that matter).

Of course now I've gone and made myself hungry. Think I'll go have a "serving" of cereal.

Goodnight, Dear Diary.

87. HOW SWEET IT IS

Wednesday, December 14

Dear Diary:

I am so exhausted tonight, but in a good way. Today was "day one" for my Christmas baking.
 And if I do say so myself, while I may not be the best gourmet cook in the world, I am definitely an above-average baker when I put my mind to it. There will be no "store-bought" Christmas baking at our house. No sir, we will have reindeer and Santa Claus shaped homemade sugar cookies with red and green sprinkles, bite-sized shortbread cookies shaped like Christmas trees, bells, stars and candy-canes topped with dollops of icing and toasted almonds, ginger snaps decorated with slivers of candied ginger, dream squares, lemon squares, iced apple pastries and maple-walnut fudge. There will be pecan pies, caramel pumpkin pies with real whipped cream and mincemeat tarts, all made from scratch. If there's one thing my mother taught me well, it was how to make any kind of pastry imaginable. For reasons I think you can appreciate, I just avoid cakes.
 There will be no fake goodies, nothing "organic", no whole-wheat flour or any other "healthy alternatives". You won't find anything "sugar-free", "light", "lite" or "diet" at our house over Christmas. Christmas is not the time for margarine, soy products, Splenda or aspartame.
 Christmas needs butter, brown sugar, white sugar, icing sugar, bleached flour, red and green food dye, sugar sprinkles, cream, whipped cream, vanilla, walnuts, pecans, almonds, maraschino cherries, coconut, ginger, cinnamon and yes, I even splurge on fresh ground nutmeg. Needless to say, I have to make a special "baking supplies" trip to Costco every Christmas.
 It takes me three days to bake, box and store everything. I make twelve dozen of each type of cookie, six batches of fudge, nine pies, six dishes of squares and four-dozen tarts.
 I know it sounds like a lot, but I give boxes of my baking to all our friends and relatives as Christmas gifts. Nobody has ever said, "No thanks." In fact, usually starting in November, people begin

looking for confirmation that they are still on my "list".

Nothing makes me happier than doing my Christmas baking. All day long the house is filled with Christmas music (Martin's noise-cancelling headphones are a blessing) and every square inch of surface in the kitchen and dining room is taken up with baking supplies, bowls of various concoctions, cooling trays and decorative tins lined with waxed paper. It is heaven. Sophie tells me she can actually smell my baking when she walks down the street.

I have even toyed with the idea of opening up a little bakery. Of course I tend to lose interest in baking once the three days of Christmas baking are over so, possibly not a sound business model, but for those three days - the world could be my oyster.

Goodnight, Dear Diary. And sweet dreams to everyone. I know mine will be.

88. PASS THE PRETZELS

Saturday, December 17

Dear Diary:

Tonight was Sophie and Dave's annual "Holiday Pot Luck Party".
    Despite the fact that I couldn't find my iron, which meant that I had to re-think my entire outfit at the last minute, I started out the evening in pretty good humor.
    It was basically the same thirty or so people as for the BBQ in July, all of whom we know and get along with. Tony's girlfriend Jessica looked like she was about to give birth any second, and Tony appeared to be keeping a pretty close eye on her throughout the evening. Apparently she is due "any day", and I had the distinct impression that they were actually hoping it would arrive on Christmas day. Anyway, they seemed happy, and showed everybody through their basement walkout "apartment". I have to say, I was quite impressed with the whole setup, and noticed the BabyBjorn we had given Jessica for her baby shower sitting in the corner of the nursery. But of course I knew it would all look like something out of a designer magazine, that's just Sophie, making sure everything is perfect for her boy - who still hasn't found the "right" position, although we were given to understand that he is considering any number of offers. Not my business. I suspect that will all sort itself out. Or not.
    I always enjoy the food at these parties, because everybody brings their own specialty dish. This is not a veggie dip and pretzels kind of a party. The dining room table was laden with all sorts of delicious, hot entrees, from delectable cheese and spinach lasagna to sweet and sour meatballs, homemade samosas to Pilau rice and curried chicken.
    Sophie had asked me to bring my Caesar salad, which everybody raved about, with homemade Parmesan garlic croutons, crisp bacon strips and my secret Caesar dressing. Throw in a few chunks of baguette, and it's actually a meal in itself. Of course we also brought a few decorative tins filled with samples of my Christmas baking.
    A couple of hours into the party, my evening started to take a bit of a turn when we found ourselves cornered by Charles, who was

waxing a little too poetic about the smoked salmon appetizers he and Daphne had brought. When I made it clear that I wasn't really a "smoked salmon person", he merely shifted his gaze in Martin's direction and carried on, non-stop. "Surely Martin must appreciate good smoked salmon. He is Norwegian, is he not?"

No detail about the delicacy he had "had brought in" from London for the occasion was left to our imaginations. "It's from Hansen & Lydersen of London... you must know of them. The very finest smoked salmon anywhere. Based on Hansen's wife's grandfather's old family recipe from Norway, I understand. He only uses the best salmon from the icy waters off the Faroe Islands, half way between Norway and Iceland, and cures it with hand-harvested sweet sea salt from the west coast of France. You really must try some, old chap. Each salmon is hand filleted and traditionally hung, and is both rich and incredibly delicate, with a juniper and beech smoked flavor that changes subtly as you taste slices cut from the crisp top to the velvety center."

Of course Martin's mouth was watering just at the description, but all I wanted to do was shake Charles by the shoulders and say, "Give it up, Charles! We all know you work at Walmart! You can quit pretending to be better than everybody else!"

I'd bet my house that one of his rich relatives in England had sent him the smoked salmon as a Christmas present. Had it "brought in" from London, my ass. Like he had his private jet dash over to pick it up just for Sophie's party. What a phony. I'm pretty sure the only "coupon clipping" Charles is doing these days is the one that involves grocery store flyers. Not that there's anything wrong with that, I do it myself. Although I have to confess that there's still a bit of a disconnect between my coupon clipping skills and my coupon using skills.

Anyway, that was the point at which the evening began to go downhill for me. I started finding almost everyone just slightly annoying. They all seemed to have so much going on in their lives. Every time I turned around somebody was telling a fascinating story about their job, or their vacation plans, or the third grandchild they were expecting, or their new business venture. I just felt like my life was stupid. All I could say was that we couldn't wait for the kids to come home for Christmas and that I had spent three days baking.

I don't remember last year being like this at all. Not that I was ever what anyone would have called "the life of the party", but I always had something to contribute - an interesting tidbit or two to share. This is not how Christmas is supposed to feel. Why do I feel so weird this Christmas? Weird and uncharitable. I hate myself right now.

Maybe things will get better when the kids arrive. Just six more days.

Goodnight, Dear Diary.

89. *O HOLY NIGHT* (Adolphe Adam, 1847)

Saturday, December 24

Dear Diary:

Today was awesome. Everything just feels right when the kids are back home. I haven't stopped smiling for two days.

Joey and Grace and her husband, John, arrived yesterday, as did Aksel and Camilla. We brought Mom up the day before. Like a ten-year-old with a new toy, Martin was thrilled to have the chance to show off his new Pilot when he picked the kids up at the airport.

Ever since Grace arrived, Twink won't let her out of her sight, following her around everywhere she goes, even into the bathroom. I guess she's really missed her.

Lucy, of course, is at DEFCON 1 with six "extra" people in house. She seems to be keeping a particularly close eye on John. Smart dog.

Joey has been entertaining everybody with all the stories about his work in Korea and his extensive travels. He really is a wonderful young man. We "did good", with both our kids, actually. Grace has such a nice way about her, always attentive to her grandparents, so calm and gentle; a great listener. I love having her around.

Tonight, after a light supper, we all gathered in the living room. Martin built a fire in the fireplace, and we sat down to enjoy one of the kids' favorite Christmas traditions, *National Lampoon's Christmas Vacation*. Christmas just wouldn't be Christmas without the Griswolds, cousin Eddie and Snots. Even Aksel couldn't help laughing out loud.

We finished off the evening with Christmas music, coffee and sweets and the Olsen family gift exchange. Just like when he was a kid, Joey sat himself down on the hearth beside the Christmas tree and took charge of handing out all the gifts and cracking jokes. I didn't want the evening to end. I hope we can always do this.

Probably the most touching gift I received this year was from Joey. He had taken a really nice photograph of the four of us to a Korean artist, who painted our family portrait onto a silk fan. It was beautiful. Grace and John gave us a spectacular pair of eleven-inch-high authentic German Nutcracker Hussars, one red and one black.

They make a wonderful addition to our Christmas décor, and will "guard" Rudolph on the dining room buffet every Christmas from here on in.

As for Martin, God love him, he had remembered a pair of gorgeous, dangling turquoise and silver earrings I had taken a shine to when we had stopped into a jewelry store three months ago to have his watch repaired. He looked so pleased with himself when I opened up the box that I didn't have the heart to tell him that I was no longer comfortable with wearing anything that might draw attention to my deformed earlobe. I could just imagine someone stretching out their fingers to fondle the very noticeable new earrings, "Gosh, those are amazing!" and then recoiling in horror when they saw that they were attached to a long, sagging flap of skin that used to be an earlobe. My reluctance to actually wear them aside, the truth was that I really did love the earrings, so it wasn't hard to look and sound absolutely thrilled.

There are a couple of reasons why Martin and Joey sort of expect me to get them "tall" hoodies, vests and casual shirts from J.Crew for any gift-giving occasion, and so I do. First, neither of them is much for buying clothes for themselves, and second, most "tall" men's' clothes you find in stores only come in size extra-large. They both seem to appreciate the fit, style and comfort of the J.Crew "tall" line of casual clothes. And I know, despite his general ambivalence when it comes to "soft" Christmas presents, that as long as I throw a hardware store purchase into the mix somewhere, Martin actually looks forward to getting new duds at Christmas.

When all the gifts had been passed out Martin announced that he had one more gift to give. He went down to the basement and came back up with a box with my name on it. Knowing how much I hate surprises, I couldn't believe he was doing this - and in front of everybody. But when I opened the box I just burst out laughing. It was a helmet - with the words "Ninja Granny" emblazoned across the front. Funny man. Funny, funny man. Joey had to take a picture of me wearing the helmet - for posterity, he said - but probably more like for Facebook. I hate pictures of myself. I haven't looked good in a picture for at least a decade. What the hell. In much the same way that a cloud of dust followed the Peanuts character Pig-Pen wherever he went, I have long since resigned myself to the fact that I am apparently being followed everywhere by "bad lighting".

Everybody knows that buying Christmas presents can be a joy when you are very close to the person you are buying for, or a burden when you don't really know someone well enough to get them a truly "personal" gift. So today my thoughts turned to making up a list of "fool proof" hostess, friend or acquaintance gifts that I could give with confidence. After many years of picking up last-minute boxes of hand-made soaps, scented candles and iTunes gift certificates, from now on I'm going to rely on my list instead:

1. A gift certificate to an interesting, new restaurant in town or to one of our favorite restaurants.
2. A gourmet cheese basket with a bottle or two of good wine.
3. An especially decadent box of chocolates.
4. A cashmere scarf in an up-to-date color, pattern and style.
5. A unique and beautiful Christmas tree ornament.
6. A bottle of (real) Champagne.
7. A bottle of Cognac.
8. A set of double-walled glass espresso or cappuccino glasses.
9. A gift certificate to a gourmet candy store.
10. A tin of Big Train Chai tea and all the ingredients to make Masala Chai.

Well, the children are nestled all snug in their beds, and I have to be up early tomorrow to get the turkey started. Can't wait.

Goodnight, Dear Diary, and Merry Christmas!

90. BIENVENUE

Monday, December 26

Dear Diary:

Well, today we held our annual Christmas soiree for friends and neighbors, and it was a blast.

The kids invited some of their old school friends over and they brought a level of energy and excitement to the party that you just don't get when it's only us "old folks".

The food was simple, the dress casual, and the mood very festive. I haven't laughed so much in a five-hour period in a long time. I was so happy that I even chose to find Charles amusing rather than annoying. Once we figured out that he was simply repeating in an incredulous tone everything we said to him, and adding "Is that so?" at the end, we just made a game out of catching him doing it.

"Korea, you say? Is that so?"

"At 325°, you say? Is that so?"

"A helmet, you say? Is that so?" Poor Charles. I almost gave him a hug.

But the really big news was that little Delphi was born this morning at 3:45, weighing in at seven pounds, eight ounces. Jessica is apparently doing fine. I was surprised that Sophie and Dave showed up to the party at all, but I guess it was the perfect opportunity to spread the news. Good for them. Of course Tony was a no-show, but he had much more important things on his mind - like maybe looking for a way to support his new baby? It doesn't get much "realer" than holding your baby in your arms and realizing, "This is it. I am responsible for this life."

It's so awesome having the kids here. Thank you, God.

Goodnight, Dear Diary.

91. DOWN TO TWO

Wednesday, December 28

Dear Diary:

The house feels so empty tonight.

We took the kids to the airport this afternoon. Martin spent the whole ride having a very sober discussion with Grace's husband, John, about military operations. As if the mere fact that they were all leaving wasn't depressing enough.

I feel numb. I spent a couple of hours lying down on Grace's bed with Twink. Not sure which of us misses her more. When I had a job I'd be heading back to work this week, so at least I'd have that distraction.

It's 8:30 p.m. Martin made himself a sandwich for dinner and took it into his office. I'm not hungry. I just want to go to bed. Or drown myself.

Or maybe counting my blessings would be a little more productive. And who would look after Mr. Boogie if something happened to me?

Maybe I just need a piece of fudge.

Goodnight, Dear Diary.

92. ARE YOU THE BEEF OR THE RACK OF LAMB?

Sunday, January 1

Dear Diary:

Well, another New Year's Eve bash at the yacht club has come and gone.

It really is a fun tradition, and for the past ten years or so Sophie and Dave have joined us. I wasn't sure they'd make it this year with the new baby in the house and all, but I guess they figured Tony and Jessica had it "under control".

As usual, the menu didn't disappoint. I had signed up for the beef tournedos with green peppercorn cream sauce, and Martin went with the herb-crusted rack of lamb. The appetizer was a delicate cream of celeriac soup, the side vegetables were cooked *al dente*, the baby spinach salad with strawberries and toasted almonds was to die for, and we all chose the crème caramel for dessert with espressos all around.

It was good to see a lot of old faces from the summer, and when I say "old faces" I do literally mean "old" faces. There are quite a few seriously old people who hang out at the club, and they all attend the New Year's Eve do. I can't say that I blame them. That will be us some day. The food is incredible, the live band is always entertaining, the dance floor is huge, and the view is spectacular.

When we get tired of dancing it's always fun to just sit and watch the "really old" couples cutting a rug. In what is probably best described as an annual tribute to ballroom dancing lessons and brow lifts, you can tell from the grimacing faces on the sea of old men that they are mentally counting their memorized steps while their wives flounce about them like peacocks with ear-to-ear grins fixed on their faces and eyes just a little too wide open.

I knew that Sophie would inevitably force the conversation around to New Year's resolutions at some point before midnight, so I came prepared this year.

"I'll start," she said. "This year I am going to learn how to knit."

Yikes. I did not see that coming. But from the look on Dave's face, I'm guessing he did. His face also suggested just a hint of exasperation. I think I know why. Like me, Dave must also be noticing that Sophie's "interest" in the new baby is rapidly approaching that fine line between "interest" and "obsession".

"That sounds like fun, Sophie. Is that so you can knit things for the baby?" Sometimes when you don't know what to say, it's easier to just state the obvious and frame it as a question. The most familiar examples of that technique being, "Are you not feeling well?" and "So, is that what you're wearing?"

"What about you, Dave? What's your resolution?" I asked.

"I'm thinking of getting a motorcycle," he replied with a little too much conviction. I knew it. The man is looking for an escape; a reason to get away from the house, and be alone. It has to bug him that he is still supporting his son, and now the girlfriend and the baby, with no end in sight. He's going to have to stand up to Sophie one of these days. But a motorcycle - is he also harboring a death wish?

"Wow!" Nervous laughter. "Are motorcycles dangerous?" I have the whole "state the obvious as a question" technique down to a fine art.

"Not if you know what you're doing." There would be no dissuading him. Sophie didn't appear to even be paying attention. I can tell you that if Martin were the one talking about getting a motorcycle I would be doing a lot more than just paying attention. I would be saying words. Many, many words. Serious words.

But, Dave being someone else's husband, I just said, "You guys have put some real thought into this," and moved on. "What about you, Martin? What's your resolution?"

Notwithstanding the fact that Sophie has made us go through this every year for the past ten years, I could tell from the look on Martin's face that he felt like I'd blind-sided him.

"I haven't really thought about it," he said. A statement I can guarantee was one hundred percent accurate.

"C'mon, honey. What would you like to do this year?"

"I don't know...maybe we can take a trip up the Alaska Highway. I've always wanted to do that. And with the new Pilot, we could bring Lucy with us... What do you think?"

I was stunned. Had he actually just come up with that on the spur of the moment? It was an awesome New Year's resolution.

"Do you mean it? That would be amazing!" I said, and leaned over and kissed him.

I don't know why I ever doubt Martin. He really is the best husband ever.

I had almost forgotten that I was going to have to tell them my resolution (the one I had intended as a sort of a light-hearted response to Sophie's inevitable question), when Sophie piped in, "Now it's your turn, Molly. What's your resolution?"

I didn't have anything else prepared, so I just went with my original plan. "My resolution this year is to organize a group of retirees to take weekly trips to the mall to swarm teenagers."

It sounded really stupid after Martin's great resolution, and not nearly as funny out loud as it did in my head this afternoon. Maybe it was all in the delivery. Martin and Sophie just looked at me as if they weren't sure they had heard me correctly.

"Good one," Dave said with a smirk on his face.

In appreciation for his acknowledgement of my attempt at humor, I gave him the facetious double "rock and roll" sign and said, "Born to be wild."

In hindsight, my innocent reference to Steppenwolf's biker song might have been a poor choice. The fact that Dave's kiss at midnight was a tad more "ambitious" than usual seems to suggest that he may have misconstrued my words. I wasn't actually looking to be clasped "in a love embrace". Let's hope it can be explained, as so many things can, by too much alcohol. Fortunately nobody else noticed.

Well, today was Day One of the New Year, and I have my work cut out for me. Those retirees aren't going to organize themselves.

Goodnight, Dear Diary.

93. HAVE YOU GOT ME ON SPEAKER?

Tuesday, January 3

Dear Diary:

Sarah called today to see if I wanted to go out shopping. Of course the first thing she always says is, "Have you got me on speaker?"

Why do some people get so weird about being on "speakerphone"? Of course I have you on speaker. It is a technological advancement designed to make talking on the telephone easier. I don't want to sit here holding a three-inch-wide telephone in my hand for thirteen minutes. What is it that you're planning on saying that simply "can't" be overheard? If nobody else is permitted to hear it, what makes you think I want to? And why are you telling me?

Unless you are suffering from a paranoid personality disorder, the number of reasons that might actually justify the need for you to be "taken off speaker" is really quite limited. If you fit anywhere in this list then I will take you "off speaker". Otherwise, get over yourself. Nobody cares.

1. You have an embarrassing medical condition that you need to discuss.
2. You have a humiliating confession to make.
3. You have devastating, sensitive news to reveal that will directly affect me, personally.
4. You have devastating, sensitive news about yourself that you want to keep private.
5. You have been kidnapped, and your kidnapper has advised you that he will kill you if I put you on speakerphone.
6. You are so famous that every word that comes out of your mouth is extremely valuable to tabloid magazines and you simply can't "take the chance" of having anything you say, no matter how mundane, being overheard.
7. You are under indictment and are afraid that you might inadvertently incriminate yourself on speakerphone.
8. You work for Homeland Security, the N.S.A., the C.I.A., the F.B.I., the S.E.C. or the R.C.M.P. and you "have a few questions" for me.

9. You have dialed my number by mistake.
10. You are running for office.
"You know I have you on speaker, Sarah."
"Well take me off."
"…Fine."
11. You are my sister.
Goodnight, Dear Diary.

94. THE AGING AQUARIUS

Saturday, January 7

Dear Diary:

Today was January 7th, the day when Christmas music no longer filled the house, when the turkey soup was all gone, when Martin and I packed up the Christmas tree and all the ornaments and decorations and hauled them down to the basement, when I carefully set Rudolph back on the shelf in my office cupboard and when the multi-colored outdoor lights were all turned off until next December 1st.

January 6th may be "little Christmas" or the Feast of the Epiphany, but January 7th always feels to me like *The Night The Lights Went Out In Georgia* (minus the hanging). On January 7th even shortbread cookies and mincemeat tarts suddenly lose their appeal. Now that the entire Christmas season is over I am starting to wonder if, once again, I will be paralyzed by my complete lack of agenda.

When I was working, I used to read the daily horoscopes in passing for entertainment - and then forget about them as soon as I had read them.

But now that I'm retired, I sometimes turn to my horoscope in search of a "message" that might give me some real direction. Unfortunately, my horoscope for today said, "All your energy should be devoted to having fun."

But today was "tear down Christmas" day, which is never what I would describe as "fun". Today was one of the few days this whole year when I actually had a specific job that needed doing. What was I supposed to do? Postpone "tear down Christmas" day to January 8th? I'm not a Philistine.

Undaunted, tonight I decided to look up my horoscope for tomorrow. I was hoping to see something a little bit mysterious or intriguing, maybe along the lines of, "Take advantage of the interesting offer you will receive today." Or, "Don't create feuds where none exist." Or even "Beware of men wearing masks."

Instead, my horoscope for tomorrow begins with the statement, "Be careful not to relax too much today." That should have been today's horoscope. What the heck am I supposed to do with that kind of advice for tomorrow? Go back to the craft store? I have absolutely nothing to do tomorrow. Christmas is over. The kids are gone. I have no job. The house is actually clean. I would love to be able to "not relax too much" tomorrow. I just don't see any way of avoiding it.

And as if that wasn't enough to convince me that my horoscope is just taunting me, how else am I supposed to interpret tomorrow's final bit of useless advice:

"You need to start opening up about all the projects you're working on right now, because people want to know what's got you so energized." That's just hurtful.

My only "projects" for tomorrow are to start on the book of Crossword puzzles I got in my stocking and to figure out what to make for dinner, neither of which I was feeling all that bad about until I read the horoscope.

Stupid horoscope. If you can't rely on your horoscope for a bit of thought-provoking advice, what can you rely on? Fortune cookies?

Hmm…maybe I'll order Chinese for dinner tomorrow.

Goodnight, Dear Diary.

95. TIME TO SAY GOODBYE

Friday, January 13

Dear Diary:

When I was heading out to the grocery store this afternoon, I picked up my keys out of the wooden bowl on the secretary in the front hall when, for no apparent reason, I was suddenly struck by how light my keychain was. I had to look twice to check that they were my keys. Let's see…car key and…house key. Yep. That was it. Car key and house key. What a sad, little key chain.

    I don't know why it has never struck me before now, because I haven't had any more than those two keys on my keychain since I retired. But today was the first time I ever had any feelings at all about how light it was. Today, I felt a real pang in my heart, almost a sense of loss.

    I remember how annoying I used to find it when the same keychain also held my building key, the key to the front door of our offices, my office door key, my desk keys and my cabinet keys. Every time I put my car key in the ignition I used to curse the heavy dangling chandelier of keys that would get all jammed together in weird ways so that I couldn't even turn the ignition key until I unstuck everything. Kind of like the gold and silver chains we wear around our necks that become mysteriously tangled in knots when they've been left in the jewelry box too long.

    But my keychain is no longer a problem. Now, I have only two keys. I can remember a time when people used to joke about how a person's importance was directly proportional to the number of keys on their keychain. Guess I'm not that important any more.

    When I got home from the grocery store, I decided that maybe it was time for my wallet to also make a clean break from everything still lingering around from my working life. There was the loyalty card from the coffee shop in our lobby that would never again owe me my tenth coffee for free. The special discount card we all had from the dry cleaning establishment down the street that was one of our best clients. The business cards I had hung onto in my wallet from people who might have turned out to be good contacts if I were still working. The dental plan card that I had been so grateful for all those years when I was employed. I have a new one now, but it's not quite the premium plan I once had. The small, laminated card with all the managers' office and home telephone numbers on it that I had carried for "emergencies". The laminated card with all of the combinations for the padlocked cabinets in the office. My rarely used free membership card to the health club on the top floor of our building. Even a few old "drink tickets" from our annual barbeque.

As semi-traumatic as the whole experience was, it sort of felt good in a way, like an acceptance that the past is the past. Some would call it "closure". Saying goodbye to all those trappings of my former working life didn't change anything, it was just a symbolic synchronization of my headspace with the fact that I had given up that part of my life almost a year ago. Hmm. Today was Friday the 13th. Maybe I should have re-thought my timing. Too late now.

I spent the rest of the day picking that annoying hard plastic thread out of all my clothing labels. Something I had always meant to get around to. New life. New priorities.

Goodnight, Dear Diary.

96. OUCH!

Monday, January 16

Dear Diary:

Okay. Martin is not, generally speaking, a whiner. But for whatever reason, today he must have told me at least a dozen times how "It hurts every time I rotate my jaw back and forth." And of course it was never enough to simply tell me that it hurt every time he "rotated his jaw back and forth", he actually had to give me a demonstration. Every time.

"See. If I go like this…Ouch!"

"Honey. Just watch. It's when I do this…Owww!"

Not that I didn't appreciate the "demonstration" the first time. I was actually curious as to what he even meant by "rotating his jaw back and forth". And, after the first demonstration I can say with absolute certainty that I, personally, have never, in the almost sixty-one years that I have been alive, had any reason to ever do anything with my jaw that even remotely resembled what Martin was trying to do. Not even at the dentist. Which, of course, begged the question, "Why are you doing that?"

"That's not the point!" he snapped. My thinking was, "…er…it kind of is, actually," but I could see that there would be no possible upside to pursuing that line of reasoning.

So I tried sympathy. "Oh, honey. That must be really painful. Do you want some ice for that?"

"Yes, of course it's painful! That's what I've been trying to tell you!"

Then I tried taking him seriously. "Do you want me to call the doctor?"

"No! He'll probably just prescribe pain pills!"

"Should I take you to Emergency for an x-ray?"

"No! I'm not going to waste a whole day sitting in an Emergency room!"

I was stumped. No ice, no doctor, no pain pills, no x-ray.

Then it came to me. Poor Martin. He has always been so fit and healthy. He can still run ten kilometers, bench press a hundred pounds, dance until dawn, slalom down the black diamond slopes and swim across a lake.

But for some weird reason, today, probably without even thinking about it, he had "rotated his jaw back and forth" and inadvertently produced the first sign of physical frailty that he had ever experienced. That was why he was so upset.

And, as unnecessary a skill as "rotating your jaw back and forth" might ever be to him for the rest of his life, he didn't like the fact that he had discovered a physical feat (obscure though it may be) that he was incapable of performing without producing pain. To him, it represented vulnerability, a chink in the armor, an Achilles' heel.

Welcome to the human race, Martin. And fasten your seatbelt. It's going to be a bumpy ride from here on in.

What I really wanted to do was give him the advice that I have chosen to live by since I hit menopause. If something only hurts "when you do it", try this: stop doing it! A couple of years ago I went ten full months without even once raising my left arm above shoulder height.

But instead, I decided to help him.

"Maybe you better not do that any more for today. You might have inflamed your jaw and be making it worse. Let's get you some aspirin for the inflammation. I'm sure it'll be better in a day or two."

I could see that he was satisfied that I had come up with a reasonable explanation. Yeah. That was it. He wasn't getting old. He just had "a little inflammation". Men.

Goodnight, Dear Diary.

97. MAN VS. FRIDGE

Friday, January 20

Dear Diary:

Why is it that when a man opens a refrigerator or a kitchen food cupboard, it is as if he has lifted the veil to another dimension filled with mysterious, alien life-forms that he finds impossible to identify?

It probably all starts with the fact that he doesn't actually want to open the refrigerator or a kitchen food cupboard in the first place.

What he really wants is for you to anticipate when he might feel like eating, retrieve all of the necessary ingredients to create something he might like to eat, and then prepare it and serve it to him without him ever having to set foot in the kitchen.

"Oh hi, honey. Thought you might feel like a pastrami on rye with a side of coleslaw and dill pickles."

Or, "I'm making some grilled cheese sandwiches with bacon. Would you like one?"

But when you have failed in your duties, and none of his "go-to" foods (apple, banana, cookie, or single-serving yoghurt) are going to quite cut it for him, he might actually find himself standing and staring into the open refrigerator or food cupboard which, if you're paying attention, is really just your cue to fix him something sensible to eat.

If you still fail to get the message, he will pretend to be looking for an item that he thinks he could manage to "prepare" himself (should it come to that) and then he will simply add the name of that item to the following question, "Where's the …?"

And so the dance begins.

"Where's the hot mustard?"

"It's there, in the refrigerator."

"Where in the refrigerator? I can't find it."

"It's on the top shelf in the door."

"No, it's not there. I looked."

You will get up and go to the open refrigerator in front of which he is still standing and staring. You will pluck the little jar of hot mustard from its place on the top shelf in the refrigerator door, exactly where you said it was, and hand it to him. He will state the obvious. "Oh. I didn't see it."

Silently, you will go back to what you were doing. About thirty seconds later he will say, "Are we out of pumpernickel?" The bad wife will pretend not to hear him. The good wife will get up again, retrieve the pumpernickel, tell her husband to go and sit down and make him the sandwich.

I have thought about this a lot, and I have come to the conclusion that there really is a logical explanation for why some men have a complete and utter inability to "see" food items in the refrigerator or the food cupboard that are sitting in plain sight, directly in front of their eyes.

Of course none of this applies to the single man, or to the man who has a "flair" in the kitchen and actually delves into the art of cuisine now and again.

But I'm talking about the rest of the men in the world, the men whose wives plan the food menus, go to the grocery store and purchase the food, put the food away in the refrigerator and cupboards, prepare all of the meals and clean up and put away all of the food afterwards.

These are the men who don't "see" the items staring them in the face because they actually have no idea what food looks like in its natural state; be it raw, in a package, a jar or a container of any sort. They have only ever seen food in its fully prepared and served state.

They know there is something called "pita crisps" that you place beside their bowls of soup, they simply don't have the remotest idea of what a "container" of pita crisps might look like in the cupboard. In fact they wouldn't even be one hundred percent sure that the cupboard would be where one would find pita crisps. Maybe they're in the refrigerator.

These men relate to food items the way children relate to Christmas presents. They love them, they just don't know or really care "where they come from".

To expect them to be capable of retrieving cilantro from the refrigerator when, as far as they are aware, cilantro is just that thing that their wife tells them is in the salad that they like so well, is actually bordering on foolishness, if not actual cruelty.

And can we really find fault when a can of tuna fish in the cupboard bears absolutely no resemblance to the tuna salad that ends up in the tuna melts that you prepare for him with shredded cheese on top?

In short, they can't find anything because they have no idea what anything looks like in its unprepared state.

So, the next time your husband says, "Honey, where's the ... ," show him some understanding. And remember - the day will come when you will need that pair of needle-nosed pliers from the garage.

Goodnight, Dear Diary.

98. TROUBLE IN RIVER CITY

Sunday, January 22

Dear Diary:

Well, I spent most of today consoling Sophie. Apparently, Jessica has taken the baby and moved back in with her mother.

The only person who is likely to be feeling any sense of relief about the situation is Dave. I suspect that the motorcycle purchase will be put on the back burner, at least for now. Sophie is devastated. Mostly for Tony, but I think also a little bit for herself.

Unfortunately, the rest of us can only be here for them and listen. This is not a time for giving advice or saying, "I told you so." Especially when you never told them what you thought in the first place. Life can be so complicated.

And the sadness they are going through right now got me thinking about the five stages of grief; denial, anger, bargaining, depression and acceptance. Which, in turn, got me wondering whether or not there are actual emotional stages to retirement.

When I look back on the past year, I can say with certainty that there was a well-defined first stage, which was a tremendous sense of relief. Man, that felt good. All the pressures and stresses of the job were gone in an instant. Not my problem anymore. No alarm clock, no racing around in the morning, no rush-hour, no clients, no meetings, no deadlines to meet, no mental gymnastics, no time-sheets, no worrying about billings or the "bottom line". It makes me smile just thinking about it.

Unfortunately, that sense of relief very quickly gave way to the onset of incredible fatigue. It was like my body was trying to make up for thirty-five years of sleep deprivation - all at once. I don't remember ever feeling so tired as I did those first several months of retirement. There was no way to just "snap out of it". It had a grip on me that was impossible to ignore. I had so much free time, but no energy to do anything constructive with it. The deep fatigue felt like it lasted a long time, and even when I was alert, my brain seemed to get hijacked by weird, random fragments of thoughts about insignificant things. Ideas that I wouldn't have wasted ten seconds on when I was working were suddenly compelling my deepest concentration and analysis. Although I'm more or less over the deep fatigue, I don't know that my brain will ever stop obsessing about the minutiae.

I wouldn't say that any of the next stages involved anger, so much as a mind-numbing boredom, leading to self-loathing, mixed with occasional feelings of resentment. And remnants of all of those feelings still linger, even rear their heads every now and again.

But life goes on, and eventually you can't help but get caught up in all the things that always made up your life outside of the workplace. It is those things, those relationships, those responsibilities, those moments of worry and moments of joy, that gradually level you off, until you turn around one day and discover that you are, actually, living your life. This is your life. It's always been there; it had just been overshadowed by your working life for thirty-five years and then by the loss of that life.

So now is the time to re-focus, to recognize who I am and to stop concentrating on what I was. And, while it may take some getting used to, this new life, it's mine. All mine.

Goodnight, Dear Diary.

99. HOW TO RECOGNIZE THAT YOU ARE RETIRED

Wednesday, February 1

Dear Diary:

I've been thinking a lot about the fact that in a few days I will have been officially retired for a whole year.

And it strikes me that, while retirement has been traditionally perceived to be a voluntary state of affairs, there are many circumstances in which people find themselves wondering whether or not they are retired because they are in a situation that looks and feels like retirement without it ever having been a conscious decision. Conversely, many people have made the conscious decision to retire, but then find themselves otherwise involved in the "working world" on an ongoing basis for any number of reasons. All of which is to say, there are a lot of people in weird positions that defy precise definition.

Think about anyone over the age of sixty who has either officially retired from, quit or lost their job. Then factor in whether or not they are actively looking for work, have given up trying to find employment, have taken on a part-time job or are considering starting up their own business. There are some situations in which it is not as easy as it might seem to answer the simple question, "Am I retired?"

And so I have come up with a set of very simple guidelines to help answer that question. Note, however, that these guidelines in no way purport to answer the somewhat similar but far more complex question, "Can I retire?"

Chances are that you are actually retired if:

1. You have ever written "good bowel movement" on your list of accomplishments for the week.
2. You are referring to your teeth when you talk about your new "implants".
3. You have stopped tweezing your grey hairs.
4. At least twice a week you have to ask someone the question, "What day is it today?"
5. You are currently wearing the clothes you wore to bed last night.

6. You are never one hundred percent sure when you've burped, that you haven't also farted at the same time.

7. You spend more time worrying about "bladder control" than "bad hair".

8. You have looked at a photo of yourself in the last six months and wondered, "Is this going to be my Obituary photo?"

9. When you get up in the middle of the night to pee, you also make a snack and turn on the T.V.

10..You remember drinking a beer while watching Richard Nixon wave goodbye on the White House lawn on August 9, 1974.

I can't stress enough that these are merely guidelines for those of you who are not quite sure whether or not you are retired, or just tired; whether or not you are retired, or the long weekend has just been super boring.

While fatigue and boredom may, indeed, be hallmarks of retirement, they are not actual signs of "being" retired, so look at the list of guidelines carefully, and if you can tick off at least three, they are probably not expecting you back at work. Congratulations!

Goodnight, Dear Diary.

100. *ANNUS HORRIBILIS?*

Sunday, February 5

Dear Diary:

I remember Queen Elizabeth II remarking that 1992 was an *annus horribilis*. And when I think back on my first year of retirement, I guess there were times when I would have said that I was having a "horrible year".

But, today was my birthday, I have been retired for exactly one year, and I think that I have finally started to appreciate my life just the way it is. There are even times when I wonder how I ever fit a full-time job into my life.

You might say that retirement is more like highway driving than the city-driving world of work. Things go better when you just sit back, relax, and enjoy the ride. I've finally stopped feeling like I'm in the middle of a "recess" that's gone on too long, and decided that it's okay to sidle to the beat of my own drum.

In fact, my year of retirement experience has led me to come up with a list of ideas and beliefs that I think capture the zeitgeist of the "age of retirement", and hope will prove valuable to anyone approaching or entering it:

1. Yes, your job felt like it was your life. But it wasn't. It was just your job. You did not die. You just don't have that job anymore. Everything else that was in your life is still there. Now you can concentrate on that. So get on with it.

2. Embrace your limitations, be they physical, financial or intellectual. Whether it is, "Oops. Sorry. I forgot," "No, I can't afford it," or even "My arthritis is acting up - maybe some other time." So long as they are used sparingly, these statements can work to your advantage.

3. Play golf, go to "trivia night" at your local pub or invest in box sets of your favorite TV series and subscribe to Netflix. "Fun" used to be the thing you could only do when you weren't working. As difficult a concept as it is to wrap your head around, now you are allowed to "have fun", however you define it, as often as you want and when you want. You don't have to impress anybody any more. So don't feel guilty about actually enjoying yourself.

4. Buy a Day Planner and fill it in. Not with things that you have to do, but with things you would like to do. It's okay to include "talk to my brother" (set aside five minutes), "talk to my sister" (set aside an hour), "download some music", "read a bit", "grout the bathtub", "spend quality time with the cat" or even "take a nap". Then feel free to scratch out anything you don't feel like doing. Remember, you're not competing for a "fully satisfactory" annual appraisal anymore.

5. Try to keep in mind that medical appointments are not your life, even if it starts to feel that way. They are still nothing more than appointments on your agenda; things to "fit in" to the rest of your life.

6. You don't have to join anything. You can, you just don't have to feel obliged.

7. Don't torment yourself by applying for jobs you find in the newspaper that are "right up your alley". You are probably over sixty. Nobody really wants to hire you and, quite frankly, you don't really want to fight traffic any more. So knock it off. If you find yourself bored, look for projects that intrigue you, not jobs.

8. Don't fall into the trap of feeling that you have to become a professional volunteer. By all means, volunteer if you want. It can be a great way to keep busy and meet new people on top of doing some good for somebody else. But take that step slowly. And be selective. Make yourself "whole" first. Don't let anybody pressure you into feeling you have an obligation to "contribute". You have already contributed plenty to society. And your time does have value. It's up to you to decide, in your own time, if, when and to whom you want to give your time and talents.

9. Do pick up an older dog from a local shelter. It will make you smile. It will make the dog smile. You will definitely feel needed. You will feel unconditional love. You will get exercise. You will feel young again. The time will fly by. And you are always going to be way smarter than your dog (unless it's a German Shepherd).

10. Never forget that when your pants start to feel uncomfortable there is an easy solution – buy bigger pants.

11. Finally, and perhaps most importantly, laugh at all the things in life that are just plain funny, even when one of those things is you. Laugh long. Laugh loud. Laugh hard. Then laugh some more. Saint Peter is never going to condemn you for "too much laughing". By

the time you have retired you should already know that mood is a choice, and it never pays to take your situation, your life or yourself too seriously. Trust me. Nobody else does.

Retirement can be weird. Retirement can be wonderful. Like many things in life, it will never be exactly what you thought it would be. Throughout our lives, we all face life-changing events that force us to re-adjust our expectations every now and again. So it should come as no surprise that, just as with marriage, divorce, childbirth, illness, job promotion, job loss, good fortune and bad, retirement requires work if we want to find our equilibrium. It's just another part of life.

And what a life it is. Sophie and Dave hosted my birthday party tonight.

From what I gather, Tony has apparently pulled himself together and starts work at the John F. Kennedy Presidential Library and Museum in Boston two weeks from Monday. As it turns out, he really was "weighing" offers all that time. I understand he was over at Jessica's mom's place tonight telling them all about his plans and trying to persuade Jessica to give him another chance. Something tells me it will all work out. Good for Tony. Of course Sophie will need more consoling, but at least her boy won't be living too far away. (Like, say Germany or South Korea, just as a couple of examples.)

All in all, we had a really lovely evening; highlighted by the most amazing coconut cream cake I have ever seen or tasted in my entire life, and a champagne toast to me. Sophie makes awesome cakes.

But the best surprise of all was Martin's present. I should stop being so reluctant to receive surprise gifts - at least from Martin - he hasn't disappointed me yet.

After the champagne toast, he handed me two boxes with silver wrapping paper and glittery purple bows attached. He wanted me to open the small box first. It was a beautiful amethyst bangle bracelet - my birthstone. "It's gorgeous!" I said as I slipped it over my wrist.

The large box was about the size of a toaster oven, but felt very light. I couldn't even imagine what would be inside. I tore through the paper and opened the box. It was filled with silver and purple crinkle paper. At the bottom, I found two envelopes, marked "1" and "2". "You have to open them in order." Martin warned.

The envelope marked "1" was thicker. Inside, was a map of The Gold Rush Route marked in red, showing the drive up through British Columbia and the Yukon into Alaska. There was also a copy of The Milepost guide for the drive.

"Wow! We're really going? This is great! When?"

"You'll need to open the second envelope." was all he said.

There was a letter inside addressed to Martin's business associates. It read:

"Please be advised that I will no longer be providing software development and consulting services to your organization as of Monday, May 1, 2017, the effective date of my retirement."

Sincerely,
Martin Olsen

ABOUT THE AUTHOR

Gwynneth Mary Lovas has been a member of the Law Society of Upper Canada since 1982, and spent the last twelve years of her legal career as a Department of Justice Senior Counsel providing advice to the Department of National Defence and the Canadian Forces. She currently works as a writer, lecturer and consultant, and is the author of *Canadian Military Law: Morale and Welfare Operations* (Carswell, 2013).

www.ingramcontent.com/pod-product-compliance
Lightning Source LLC
Chambersburg PA
CBHW071700090426
42738CB00009B/1606